Praise

Sharp, insightful and highly amusing ... so entertaining, you don't realise how much you're learning. * * * * * 5 stars!

Ian George, Executive President Marketing, Paramount Pictures International

Richard Hall's book doesn't lie. It is brilliant! Read this book. It is stimulating, entertaining and nutrient rich. Written in an engaging and inspiring style, it is packed with ideas and examples and is a must for grads and seasoned marketers alike.

Tom Hings, previously Director, Brand Marketing, Royal Mail

Brilliant Marketing reflects all I know of Richard: not only is he a man of great humour and wisdom, but his belief in the endless possibilities of people's potential shines through. Use this book to challenge yourself and the 'right way of doing things' – Richard will show you that the only barriers to success are lack of self-belief and passion for your brand.

Rupert Maitland-Titterton, Cluster Leader Communications North Europe, Tetra Pak

I'm a huge fan of both Richard's writing and wisdom. This book is packed with brilliant nuggets that offer the kind of insight that will transform your understanding of the marketing mix and allow you to harness its potency. A must-read for anyone about to engage with this industry.

Rachel Bell, founder, Shine Communication

Brilliant Marketing is the antithesis of many a marketing textbook. Hall backs up his claims that the business of marketing should be a roller coaster, with a high-speed tour of what makes this profession great.

Will Arnold-Baker, Managing Director, Publicis

brilliant

brilliant
marketing

PEARSON

At Pearson, we believe in learning – all kinds of learning for all kinds of people. Whether it's at home, in the classroom or in the workplace, learning is the key to improving our life chances.

That's why we're working with leading authors to bring you the latest thinking and best practices, so you can get better at the things that are important to you. You can learn on the page or on the move, and with content that's always crafted to help you understand quickly and apply what you've learned.

If you want to upgrade your personal skills or accelerate your career, become a more effective leader or more powerful communicator, discover new opportunities or simply find more inspiration, we can help you make progress in your work and life.

Pearson is the world's leading learning company. Our portfolio includes the Financial Times and our education business, Pearson International.

Every day our work helps learning flourish, and wherever learning flourishes, so do people.

To learn more, please visit us at **www.pearson.com/uk**

brilliant

brilliant
marketing

Second edition

Richard Hall

Harlow, England • London • New York • Boston • San Francisco • Toronto • Sydney • Auckland • Singapore • Hong Kong
Tokyo • Seoul • Taipei • New Delhi • Cape Town • São Paulo • Mexico City • Madrid • Amsterdam • Munich • Paris • Milan

PEARSON EDUCATION LIMITED

Edinburgh Gate
Harlow CM20 2JE
United Kingdom
Tel: +44 (0)1279 623623
Web: www.pearson.com/uk

First published 2009, 2010 (print and electronic)
Second edition 2012, 2013 (print and electronic)
Rejacketed edition 2015 (print and electronic)

© Pearson Education Limited 2010, 2015

ISBN: 978-1-292-08106-9 (print)
          978-1-292-08448-0 (PDF)
          978-1-292-08449-7 (eText)
          978-1-292-08458-9 (ePub)

British Library Cataloguing-in-Publication Data
A catalogue record for the print edition is available from the British Library

Library of Congress Cataloging-in-Publication Data
A catalog record for the print edition is available from the Library of Congress

10 9 8 7 6 5 4 3 2 1
18 17 16 15 14

Series cover design: David Carroll & Co

Print edition typeset in 10/14pt Plantin MT Pro by 71
Print edition printed and bound in Great Britain by Henry Ling Ltd, at the
Dorset Press, Dorchester, Dorset

NOTE THAT ANY PAGE CROSS REFERENCES REFER TO THE
PRINT EDITION

Contents

Author's acknowledgements

The changing world of marketing

In a changing world where people's expectations are rapidly changing and where economic train crashes are a matter of normality, marketing has never been more important. This book is pretty much a rewrite of the one I wrote in 2008 as Lehman Brothers collapsed and the world became a chillier place.

If you enjoyed that first version you'll find this one recognises the needs of these times and the constant demand to do more with less.

Thank you

Thank you to my long-suffering wife who has an astute eye for good design and can spot bullshit a mile away. That's a big help when writing about marketing.

Thank you to Eloise Cook, my commissioning editor, who has patience, insight and enthusiasm in equal and helpful measure.

Thank you to the Pearson team and especially for getting my books into so many interesting places – they are now published in some 22 countries.

Thank you to that band of colourful thinkers who inspire me: James Arnold-Baker, Penny Hunt, Seamus Smyth, Roger Alexander, Daryll Scott, Peter Lederer and many others.

And thank you those who read me and react to what I say. The marketers of today and tomorrow are the key architects of the world we are creating.

Who am I?

I spent my early career at Reckitt's, RHM and Corgi Toys before going into the lovely world of advertising at French Gold Abbott, FCO (where I had the best time in my life until now) and finally at Euro RSCG.

Now I mentor many key executives, run my own consultancy, chair several companies and live in Brighton surrounded by family and grandchildren. I watch the firework display that is today's global economy with amazement and delight. Life is never boring. And it just keeps on getting better.

Finally, I love the discipline and the art of marketing. I hope you begin to see why and that you share this love as you read this book.

www.colourfulthinkers.com

http://marketing-creativity-leadership.blogspot.com

richard@hallogram.freeserve.co.uk

Publisher's acknowledgements

We are grateful to the following for permission to reproduce copyright material:

Chapter 4, overview of the Nike story adapted from Nike Culture, by Robert Goldman and Stephen Papson, SAGE Publications (© Goldman, R. and Papson, S. 1998) is reproduced by permission of SAGE Publications, London, Los Angeles, New Delhi and Singapore; Chapter 5 extract abridged from Emma Haslett, 'Two Topman T-shirts trigger Twitter tirade', Management Today, 14 September 2011 reproduced from Management Today magazine with the permission of the copyright owner, Haymarket Business Publications Limited; Chapter 6, extract from 'The Strange Death of Modern Advertising' from Financial Times, 22 June 2006 with permission from Lord Maurice Saatchi and the Financial Times.

In some instances we have been unable to trace the owners of copyright material and would appreciate any information that would enable us to do so.

Preface

What is marketing about?

In my last edition of this book I said marketing was about the art of seduction. In a way I wish I hadn't done so because I made it all sound a bit too tabloid. Marketing is more serious than that, and these are serious times. Marketing is about the skilful art of creating and building relationships between a brand or a company and its consumers, customers and stakeholders.

Marketing is about the art of informing and persuading. It's about creating conversations. It's about maximising the effectiveness and the efficiency of achieving sales. It lies at the very heart of any business. In a company of any scale, that company will fail if the CEO isn't constantly attuned to and in control of its marketing.

In a small company or a start-up the reason a company fails is likely to be one of three:

1 inferior product

2 cash flow problems

3 poor marketing.

When marketing really works you know it – sales go up, share goes up, research tells you that it's working, you get write-ups in marketing magazines and there's a buzz about. But it's also fun because marketing deals with what makes people tick. And what is more fun than being with and relating to people?

The world has changed. So marketing has to as well.

Still the most potent words you'll see in-store are 'new improved', which means good old values but better performance. That's what this book is ... new, improved. And that's what all brilliant marketing needs to be.

Marketing is at the centre of the commercial stage as everyone realises that the chase for sales growth or, perhaps more realistically, business survival is something brilliant marketers who really understand their trade customers and their end consumers can achieve and no one else can.

To keep up with the 'new improved' brilliant marketing you have to not just have your finger on the pulse of the modern world, you have to tightly embrace the changes within it:

1   Innovation is expected the whole time – same-old, same-old will die.

2   New technology is a friend – use it, don't be in awe of it.

3   There are specific demographic segments of key interest – Generations Y and Z; the young-elderly; the leading-edge colourful thinkers.

4   Embrace psychographics – what sort of people are you targeting? What turns them on (and off)?

5   Consumers are getting smarter, so be innovative in the way you talk to them.

6   If you aren't being creative and exciting you deserve to fail.

Whether you are already in marketing (or thinking about it) or are intrigued by the subject as an outsider, welcome to the strong alcohol of 'brilliant marketing'. Marketing is a fuel that can really transform things. Let's start by looking at some great stories to see just how enthralling marketing can be.

Marketing stories – gather round, people

brilliant example

I love my Apple

Apple was nearly bust a decade ago. And then Steve Jobs who'd founded the company and had been ousted returned. He diagnosed the problems. Apple had a long, dull product line, terrible logistics and was a challenger brand whose biggest enemy was itself. Michael Dell actually thought Apple should shut down, it was that bad. Jobs shortened the line radically, insisted the products became 'sexy', launched the living poster sites of Apple Stores and went on a crazy crusade of relentless improvement. As an astute marketer who never used research to tell him what people would like, Jobs understood that he was in the consumer appliance business, not the computer business. He made people around him do simple things brilliantly. Apple is a legend as a leader of markets that never stops trying to do it better – or faster – or lighter – or brighter. When Jobs said to John Sculley (then at Pepsico) 'Do you want to spend your life selling sugared water or do you want to try and change the world?' he was showing himself to be a great salesman and a visionary. Apple actually has changed the world.

brilliant example

Happy cows. Great ice cream.

The launch of Ben & Jerry's ice cream (now owned by Walls, a division of Unilever) had great PR – we all knew that it was owned, and that the various tastes were created, by the eponymous couple of rebels with long beards, both with hippy attitudes and both lovers of organic food. The product design was fun and exciting and not corporate in feel. The philosophy was encapsulated by an advertisement on the London

▶

Underground that proclaimed 'Mission statement: To make nice ice cream'. What more can you say? How great to ridicule 'mission statements'. And they are still having fun with the brand, declaring on their web site their adherence to 'peace, love and ice cream' and in their crusade to create a 'caring dairy, milking happy cows, not the planet'. Rock on!

Marketing makes me smile

I like shopping. I like new products. I love quirky stuff. I love the National Trust doorstop that is a life-size hare. I love Hotel Chocolat's Chilli Chocolate. I love the storage boxes in Selfridges that are each decorated with a different pantone colour. I love Rymans ... all those useful office things.

And I love the Google logo: colourful, three-dimensional, and through Dennis Hwang's Google Doodles it is topical too. The 'doodles' are the inventive way he plays with the logo on special anniversaries so you have the sense that the brand is constantly being refreshed.

I suppose I'm a marketing junkie but in truth isn't the enthusiasm of marketing precisely what makes New York, Hong Kong or Borough Market so exciting? Give me a busy street full of shops trying new stuff rather than any museum or art gallery.

There isn't time NOT to be brilliant at marketing

Many people seem to feel too busy to even try and be brilliant nowadays. If a deadline is more important than the quality of what is done by that deadline we are doomed. Despite the improvements in technology we have less time than ever. All executives are on 24/7/365 with smartphones. We simply have to find time to be more creative if we want to shine in marketing. This is not just a skillset thing, it's a mindset thing too. We have to find ways of maximising the stimuli to creative brilliance. As Maurice (now Lord) Saatchi said:

'Creativity is the last legal way to gain an unfair advantage.'

This book is a manifesto for brilliance, the kind of brilliance that comes from an intuitive leap that all brilliant marketers make in working out how to get their target consumers to do and think something they otherwise wouldn't have thought about or done. Brilliant marketing is that magic stuff, the ideas, the actions and the campaigns that make a real difference.

This is not, finally, a textbook. It is not a business book either, although it is about business.

It's a thriller, pure and simple.

PART 1

Putting marketing into context

This book teaches those who want to do it and those who want to understand it how marketing works in today's economy. Before we get down to the nitty-gritty of the tools of marketing, it's important we know how to get in the right frame of mind, that we understand the essence of marketing.

CHAPTER 1

Marketing brilliance starts with a sense of smell

S herlock Holmes enters stage left.

Any of the great detectives would have been good at marketing because they'd have been temperamentally adept at the first thing that matters, finding out 'whodunit'. Just as a city trader, presumably, has a nose for the market, its shifts and swings, so the marketer, just as skilled and arguably more useful, can smell gaps in markets, opportunities to position a brand to best advantage, the charm to engage a potential customer in a mutually interesting conversation and a voracious appetite to win market share.

Most of all, do you have a nose for this? Can you be like Helena Rubinstein who, on being asked how she'd chosen her new perfume, said, immortally, 'because it smells of money'?

brilliant tip

Use all your senses, not just your brain.

This changing world

The world in which we now live will be tougher than the heady days of the early and mid noughties, tougher but more exciting. Getting a sale is going to be harder. And when marketing people talk about sales more than they talk about image you know times are tough. But all we have to do is work harder and smarter. Three things are now at the top of any marketing agenda:

1 How good is our relationship with our customers?

2 What's the value for money of our products or services really like in the marketplace?

3 Are our customers hearing us? Are they listening to us? Are they engaged by us?

brilliant tip

Marketing must be exciting. Today we have a whole new set of tools available, which means we can communicate more sharply and vividly.

How to focus

● Most marketing textbooks don't help. They are not bad books but they offer ordinary solutions and are boring. They tell you too much in a dull drone.

● Always have a list of 'must dos' on your desk.

● Put away your calculator. Marketing has more to do with art than science, more to do with feelings than logic.

> Marketing has more to do with art than science, with feelings than logic.

Here's the hierarchy of talent: mindset first; skillset second; smart-set third. How you feel; what you know; how you utilise both together. Getting it together is the way to focus.

brilliant tip

Marketing has more to do with feelings than logic so try to go with the way you feel instinctively. Let your gut have a vote. Guts are critical to brilliant marketing.

● Have a go. Focus on 'doing things'. I love seeing people do clever things, such as Nestlé's launch of it's Skinny Cow Hot Chocolate drink. The brand was targeting young women who loved fashion but had limited budgets. So it was showcased in Oxford Street and Manchester, at House of Fraser boutiques and at tasting sessions at George at Asda (the biggest UK clothes retailer). Lesson: focus on your core market and be there when they first encounter your brand.

● Curiosity is a tool. Having it makes you focus on asking 'Why?' Spend time scanning the web, reading papers, looking at magazines, visiting shops and talking to bright people. Being good at marketing is like still being at university, but with less lager.

● Excess thinking leads to daydreaming. Think in a step-by-step way. Don't think too big, don't think too small, don't think too much. Focus on trying to understand your customer. Feel the momentum of a market and try to work with it rather than analysing every last bit of data. Focus on trying to understand your customer – that's the real key.

● Gather round and listen to more stories. Stories are historically how information, advice or lessons to be learned were passed down. Today they have come back in a big way. Throughout this book I use contemporary stories to illustrate the way to become a brilliant marketer.

▶ brilliant example

Nespresso

Nestlé earned its spurs by being a big, aggressive, sales-driven business with some historic brands (added to when they bought Rowntree). For many, the arrival and subsequent explosion in size of Nespresso has been a surprise. The more so, as it seems to operate as an autonomous arm of the Swiss parent. What can we learn from the marketing cocktail the people at Nespresso invented?

- They recognised the pent-up consumer demand for really good coffee. Starbucks and others give us better coffee. Nespresso gives us the best-ever coffee.
- They price it as very expensive for instant coffee but very cheap in the overall scheme of beverages.
- They deliver it to us as an easy-to-make, at-home product and give us a recycling mechanism.
- They ceaselessly innovate with new flavours.
- They give us great decaffeinated too.
- They create good partnerships with appliance manufacturers of the Nespresso machines and focus on the software – the coffee.
- They have George Clooney as a spokesman – and everyone loves George. I bet even the Pope is a secret fan.
- They make it hard to get then easy to get by saying 'to have it you must join the club and you can only do this by owning a proper Nespresso machine'. There's no entry cost but you must join to be 'allowed' to buy their coffee. Ordering is a phone call away and 24 hours later you're drinking more great coffee.
- They are very clever. They've created a luxury brand at an accessible price that is superb in quality (even Gordon Ramsay serves Nespresso).

Four lessons

1 Superior products do better (that's so obvious).

2 Pricing at a new level requires you to rethink your distribution model.

3 Sexy branding, advertising and presentation work.

4 An exclusive, luxury feel pleases – never underestimate the consumer. Mass marketing increasingly feels like a mess. We want to be treated as special. Nespresso gets this.

brilliant tip

Never underestimate your customer.

Think small

If you are a small business shaking your head thinking I'm suggesting you can marshall marketing tactics like the mighty Nestlé, well, you can in your own way. Nespresso thinks small. It loves its product. It has fun with it. Go to the very few stores where you can buy it, like Selfridges (if you are a club member), and look at the displays and the quality of the staff.

By thinking small and with such detail, by creating a virtually one-to-one customer experience, Nespresso has proved that small, beautiful and quality can also become big. The danger will be in Nespresso forgetting, with its increasing success, that its small thinking is in fact one of the keys to that success.

Change the way you look at things

People who write about marketing or management are always talking about 'change'. If you think about it, they would be out of business without the existence of unsettling and unexpected change. My next book will certainly not be called *How to keep everything exactly the same.*

The Nespresso story shows how you can change your mindset. It was not easy for the company to NOT seek grocery distribution, because that's what Nestlé does and is – a machine to drive tonnes of products into shops. Yet here Nespresso put itself where Prada and Versace sit. Here it wrote new rules. And you can too. You don't have to market what you have in the same way as your competitors do. You have permission to work out a new and a better way.

One of the things any marketer wants to be is cutting edge – why? Because innovation is more fun. But there's another reason. Being cutting edge says something about your being a modern, state-of-the-art brand.

I said don't think too much, but ponder this. How do people, in as many different markets as you can think of, do what they do? Cars, fashion, organic vegetables, wine, hammers, insurance, anything. It'll open your mind and kill the voice that says 'We always do it this way'.

Marketing – a simple plan of attack

1 **Write the marketing brief** – the discipline of setting out what you have, what makes it special and what you need to get done. This is your map.

2 **Define your resources** – who you have on your team, how much time and talent they have. Be clear about what they and you are capable of delivering. Next, how much money do you have to spend? This will determine what you can and cannot do. Never bite off more than you can chew.

3 **Examine your options** – and then settle on one. Go in one direction; don't go wandering about. So long as you

have a clear brief, then the things that most economically and effectively match the objectives you have set should be shortlisted. One word is

> Focus is the single most important quality in marketing and business.

key here: focus. Focus on what you are trying to achieve. Focus is the single most important quality in marketing and business.

4   **Write a detailed 'how-to' plan** – no one should ever spend a penny of a marketing budget without having a good robust plan. Detail really matters. Big-picture thinking alone won't pay bills.

5   **Execute that plan** – Harvard Business School say execution is more important than strategy. They have dozens of case studies where the strategy was fine and the execution was wanting. Is everything ready on time? Is everything right? This is your checklist time.

6   **Measure the results** – everything you do must have an effect. Your job is to measure these. Are sales going up? Is share going up? Is anything changing? As a result of your review does anything need changing? Go back to the brief and make sure it still holds water. Never, ever keep pouring good money after bad.

Everyone needs to understand how marketers think and what they can do for business. Marketing lies in your persona and attitude as much as in the marketing weapons available to you. Maybe marketing isn't for you, but if you work on it (and want it) you can turn yourself into a brilliant marketer. Alternatively you can learn how to work with marketers so your respective skills shine. Unfortunately some marketers today are behaving more like ordinary tradesmen than the magicians they need to be. To be brilliant our marketing people need to be inspirational, not merely adequate.

> To be brilliant our marketing people need to be inspirational, not merely adequate.

brilliant tip

Be an optimist, because the first golden rule of marketing is that 'nothing is impossible'.

Personality checklist

1 Do you love your brand?

2 Are you open-minded?

3 Are you competitive?

4 Do you make things happen?

5 Do you like people?

6 Do you have loads of energy?

7 Do you love shopping?

8 Do you dream and can you dream?

All good businessmen are jugglers

But none more so than marketing people. Marketing is an art but with a bit of science thrown in. If you are going to be as good as you can, you need to have both intuition and the ability to dissect data. You need to be an optimist and a realist. You need to know when to gamble and when to cut your losses. You need to be adept at separating wheat from chaff. This is a juggling act of time, money and resources.

And, shifting focus from office and documents to the outside world, because in a people-business brilliance can't exist behind a computer alone. We all of us spend an increasing amount of time dealing with hundreds of emails, working on spreadsheets, processing stuff. Start looking people in the eye, start inspiring and being inspired, start listening and start trying to be brilliant.

Marketing people like to take control at meetings. Meetings are great fun because they put people on their mettle. Meetings at their best are great because they are idea-generative. Meetings need to end with a burst of positivity, which marketers are good at. Remember, 'nothing is impossible' – this is the real marketing person's creed.

Too much of the world today is merely competent. It is fit for purpose. It is satisfactory. That does not make it competitive enough when others are striving for excellence. John Neill, CEO of Unipart, said of Britain in the 1980s: 'people in UK manufacturing didn't know what good was'. We didn't then, but many are now beginning to know what brilliant is. And the good news is we've always been good at marketing. The challenge now is to prove we can excel at it and get to that A* level.

brilliant tip

Imagine selling your brand to someone you've never met before. Think about how you would inspire them.

If you don't love selling, you aren't a marketer

Let's not get too technical about basic selling. In simple terms, do you like pitching and do you want to win?

Imagine the ideal state of mind: you're enthusiastic and friendly; you talk in user-friendly, non-technical language in order to reach people at their level; you show how your product solves the problem they've got; and you keep their attention. Above all, you want to show you love your product and want them to love it too.

This is about being hands-on, getting out and about, hearing, smelling and touching the world around us. Marketers need to be salespeople, bookkeepers and creative storytellers all in one. They need to be jugglers but most of all they need the instincts of the hunter-gatherer salesperson because that's when you can really smell what's going on in the market.

> Marketers need to be salespeople, bookkeepers and creative storytellers all in one.

Be a rebel

Thomas Jefferson said a bit of rebelliousness now and then did a bit of good.

Do not ever be a yes-man. If the product you are marketing needs improving, changing or even withdrawing from sale, get it done. The only place for a popularity contest is with the consumer. Your job is to be the guardian of the brand, of quality, and of that bond of trust with the end user that will keep you in business.

Being a rebel does not mean being an idiot. It means being clear about what's right and what's needed. It's about being your own man or woman. Just-get-away-with-it is not in the vocabulary of the 'brilliant marketer'.

Zig when the others zag

Be unpredictable. In GE, the huge US conglomerate, they set up a project company-wide, as the dotcom boom started, entitled 'destroyyourowncompany.com'. This was a classic piece of zigzag thinking.

So here's how to zig and to zag. Draw a line down the centre of a piece of paper. In the left-hand column write 'us'; in the right-hand column write 'our competition'. Write down your plan in summary and then what you would do to thwart it if you were the competition.

Now write down an action on your part that might really wrong-foot your competitor. For example, increasing your quality and reducing your price simultaneously, which will be painful on margin but horrible for your competitors, or increasing your price significantly and improving your service levels and positioning yourself much higher – a real premium choice, or simply increasing your marketing spend. The art of being counter-intuitive can provide dividends. Learn it and be a tricky competitor.

Are you a big brand or a little brand?

Do not fight out of your league as you won't have the resources. Read *Eating the Big Fish* by Adam Morgan to understand the role of the smaller challenger brand. The classic example of small challenger David (Avis) fighting market leader Goliath (Hertz) was in the advertising line: 'When you're only

> Being short of ammunition forces you to be clever.

number 2, you try harder. Or else.' Being short of ammunition forces you to be clever. As the scientist Lord Rutherford said, 'We have no money so we shall have to think.'

Learning from your peers and the stars

Sir John Hegarty, founder of the British advertising agency Bartle Bogle Hegarty, said:

'You must understand that I am cursed with being an incorrigible optimist ... I work because I love it. I'm genuinely interested in stuff. I love staying alert and keeping an open mind. The thing that ages you more than anything else is closing down, having a fixed point of view ... [advertising has] entered the world of fashion where creativity and innovative thinking are paramount.'

Rachel Bell is CEO of Shine Communications. She is totally convincing and committed. She has clarity, certainty and focus. With her, PR moves centre stage. No wonder Shine wins so many awards. Her big lesson is to love her clients, be in business partnership with them and be tireless in trying to improve herself, her people and her clients' sales. Listen to people like her.

Arjo Gosht who founded Spannerworks, which got really big in the digital space, and then sold it to iCrossing, is the sort of person to listen to. Search engine optimisation comes to life when he speaks.

Look at TED to see great speakers talk on a variety of subjects and study the passion and conviction with which they communicate their ideas: Sir Ken Robinson on creativity, Matt Ridley on this radically improving world and Sal Khan on mathematics. Marketing is an attitude of mind as well as a set of skills. An enthusiast who's still learning will usually outwit a cynic who's a master of technique.

What connects all these people is their hunger to win, to learn and to get something done. In my experience find a marketer and then find one who laughs, talks and does narrative – a storyteller – and listen to what they say. You'll learn loads.

> Most good marketers are the sort of optimists who seem to make their own luck.

Finally, when given a list of candidates for a vacant post, Napoleon said, 'Bring me lucky generals, not just good ones.' Energy and guessing well can lead to luck, but most good marketers are the sort of optimists who seem to make their own luck. The sun shines on them and their glasses are always half full.

brilliant tip

In marketing you have it in your power to transform a business.

How to develop your marketing muscle

Is there really such a thing as marketing muscle? Marcus du Sautoy, Professor of Mathematics at the University of Oxford, described how he, as a teenager, suddenly 'got' maths. It was, he said, like the sun coming out and a pattern emerging out of complexity.

For me it happened when I began to take data seriously and the numbers in a piece of market research (a Nielsen, Taylor Nelson or AGB tracking study) began to tell me their story. Suddenly seeing it and hearing it in your head are exciting.

You'll develop your marketing muscle and practise your marketing skills by trying to see patterns emerging from life around you. This will vary from market to market, so if you want to be a business-to-business marketer, spending long hours in Tesco or in Wetherspoons may be less helpful than going to a trade fair in Hanover.

Marketing – some useful exercises

Not everyone wants to be in marketing, not everyone has the extrovert and enquiring mind about people that being in marketing requires. However, if you are in business it's essential you understand what marketing is all about and how the marketing mindset works. Like learning a musical instrument or being good at a sport, being a master at marketing takes a lot of practice, a lot of knowledge and constant questioning. Those best at it immerse themselves in it and become addicted to it. It is more than just a job. It is a calling.

So if you want to do it, go for it. And if you don't, then try to understand those enthusiastic and energetic fanatics in your company and treat them kindly.

1 **Go shopping** to wherever products you are interested in are displayed and sold. See how the retail experts see things, where and how they are displayed, what's on promotion, what's new. Don't go to just one store, cover them all to see what the differences are. Pick up brochures.

2 **Go to trade shows** as often as you can. You'll hear more, see more and learn more than you could imagine. There are trade shows for everything, everywhere the whole time. And they are an eye-opener.

Go to them with a plan:
- What's new?

- What's being done in presentation, display and design terms that's useful to know about?
- How would you summarise the ten most important things you learn each time?

Never leave with a hazy 'it was just rather busy' impression. Remember you are in the 'specifics' business.

3 **Travel a lot.** Business expert Tom Peters said no one ever wasted money travelling. With every airport you pass through, every mainline station you get out at and every new town you visit something happens to you. You see new stuff, such as unfamiliar brands and posters, people dressed differently. As a marketer you experience a different environment in which to hold conversations with consumers. Travelling sharpens your edge.

4 **Listen more.** Listen to the radio – for me it's Radio 4, Classic FM, Radio 5 Live, Radio 2, Juice and Radio Sussex. Listen to the words people use and how language changes. Listen to DJs and to politicians. Most of all listen to anyone you can find who's in, been in or who's interested in marketing. It's a subject people like talking about. The British Chambers of Commerce, the Royal Society of Arts and innumerable marketing forums will all give you access to some interesting stuff. Avoid big expensive conferences at all costs ... these are money machines, not real ways to share ideas.

5 **Read lots of stuff.** Read the business section of your chosen daily paper to see who's doing what to whom. Check out the *Financial Times* regularly in your local library or, if you can afford to, buy it. Read *Campaign, Marketing, PR Week*. Read a select group of books that have ideas that impinge on and shape marketing thinking. Here are a few to start you off:

i)   *Freakonomics and Super-Freakonomics* by Don Levitt

ii)   *The Rational Optimist* by Matt Ridley

iii)   *Tipping Point, Blink, The Outliers, What the Dog Saw* all by Malcolm Gladwell

iv)   *Bounce* by Matthew Syed

v)   *The Walmart Effect* by Charles Fishman

vi)   *Inside Steve's Brain* by Leander Kahney

vii)   *The Google Way* by Bernard Girard

viii)   *Loose* by Martin Thomas

ix)   *The World is Flat* by Thomas Friedman

Most of all, become a great dipper in and out of books, especially in bookshops.

6   **Surf the net.** In the USA, according to a Nielsen study conducted in mid-2011, 23 per cent of the time Americans spend online is spent on social media. So you can do this, especially checking out up-to-date marketing stories on LinkedIn, but more productively overall there are four places to spend time:

i)   YouTube, where you can get to see all the best and most up-to-date TV commercials.

ii)   Fast Company, which comes out daily and has a lot of insightful articles including some on marketing issues.

iii)   TED, where you get to see the most recent speeches made at various sites around the world by smart people who have 'ideas worth spreading' (TED stands for Technology, Entertainment and Design and is the single most transformative influence on presenting in the 21st century.) And now there's 5x15 too – a similar service.

iv) Trendwatch and Springwise, which give monthly insights into new global product launches in consumer and business-to-business products and services.

Apart from that, dip around occasionally in your own sector to see what's what.

7 **Watch people.** How you develop your marketing muscle depends on how well you understand the way people think, feel, behave and buy things. Watching what people do in supermarkets, car showrooms, DIY stores, being approached by 'chuggers' in the street, at farmers' markets or trade shows give you insights into this. If you aren't interested in this topic you aren't going to enjoy marketing.

8 **Keep notes.** If you keep notes of what you see you'll build a useful archive of stuff over time. My advice is to try to keep it in one place, not on scraps of paper, and to try and be cryptic. It's more of an *aide-memoire* than a detailed record.

CHAPTER 3

The marketing battleground – past, present and future

'Battleground' sounds a bit violent. Marketing's always been a bit adversarial but as times have got so much tougher we shouldn't understate just how rough the competition is. The call for brilliance in marketing to help give a competitive edge is really intense. There's a book by Howard Stevenson called *Do Lunch or Be Lunch*. There isn't time for lunch today. We are all trying too hard to survive.

Welcome to the past

Nearly 100 years ago Henry Ford said:

'History is more or less bunk. It's tradition. We don't want tradition. We want to live in the present, and the only history that is worth a tinker's damn is the history that we make today.'

(Chicago Tribune, *1916)*

Henry was right, but he'd have been amazed at how eternal truths and tradition are being discarded today. Three years ago, of the top twelve global brands only two, Microsoft and Google, were created after 1940. By 2011 that number was six and my guess is by 2020 all twelve will be 'modern' brands, and about a third will be Chinese, Brazilian and Indian because times are changing and we are living in the present.

sermon or make a better mouse trap than his neighbour, tho'
he build his house in the woods, the world will make a beaten
path to his door.' Look at Kindle, iPad, Dyson, Bose and BMW.
Brilliant marketing today involves spending as much time wor-
rying about the product and how it looks, tastes and performs as
on considering how to market it.

We want language and relationships to be authentic

Yesterday there was subservience to the establishment.
Newscasters on TV were craven in dealing with their leaders:
'Prime Minister, sir, did you have a good holiday?'

> Today marketers have
> got to speak 'people',
> not 'corporate'.

**Today marketers have got to
speak 'people', not 'corporate'.**
Like it or not (and most senior corporate executives I talk to don't seem
to like it at all), consumers are now
in charge. They're in charge because they own today's primary
medium, the web. Companies can't control what's on there. If
you search for any company with the words 'bad news' attached
you'll find yourself getting into a morass of grumbles. BMW
may say it's a great car but ten of their angry customers can
obliterate the value of their shiny advertising in minutes.

I loved a book called *The Cluetrain Manifesto* (2000) written
by Rick Levine, Christopher Locke, Doc Searls and David
Weinberger. In it the four authors say 'talk is cheap'. And this
comes from Rick Levine, ex-Sun Microsystems, about our
having 'no choice' in the way things are:

*'People talk to each other. In open, straightforward conversations.
Inside and outside organisations. The inside and outside
conversations are connecting. We have no choice but to participate in
them.'*

For years brochure writers have been trying, in a pompous way,
to speak to their audience. But consumers today want to be

spoken to in the language of their friends, not the language of yesterday's proprietor.

brilliant tip

You need a great product but a real human being has to present it engagingly and sell it with conversational passion.

Noisy mass marketing is dead

Yesterday we interrupted people with our story. We took up a megaphone and blasted our marketing message to whoever was out there to hear it. It is what we call 'interruption marketing' and it worked because TV was cheap and because consumers put up with being interrupted.

Today we have more knowledgeable conversations. Don't for instance, imagine that Nike could have got the sports thing as right as they did if they hadn't spent a huge amount of time with athletes, soaking up locker-room gossip. Don't imagine the John Lewis Partnership could be as successful as it is without brilliant people management, which involves a high level of interest in everyone who works there. Spending money and effort on getting your staff to really know their stuff is vital.

brilliant tip

An internal love affair leads to an external communication of it.

From management to leadership to heroism

Yesterday we were in manufacture. We didn't have CEOs, we had managing directors. Leadership was something we expected from admirals and generals, not businessmen.

Inspiring leadership is on everyone's agenda. The late Steve Jobs, Larry Page, Oprah Winfrey, Martin Sorrell, Alex Ferguson and Jamsedji Tata are the heroes of the 21st century. Everyone recognises the roles of innovation and creativity. But marketing consists of creative prima donnas. To get the best out of them we need the kind of leadership seen in orchestras with the Simon Rattles of this world. Of course we need wizards, but we also need impresarios.

brilliant tip

Marketing today is about being heard through the white noise. You need to transmit at the right frequency for your audience to hear you.

Lessons on working with change

1 There's a sense of frenzy in a changing world so there are a lot of things to do at the same time.

We are all required to do more and more multi-tasking. But David Weinberger said (again in *The Cluetrain Manifesto*) that focus is in and multi-tasking is out.

'The sum total of attention is actually decreased as we multi-task. Slicing your attention, in other words, is less like slicing potatoes than slicing plums: you always lose some of the juice.'

brilliant tip

Focus is 'in': save that juice. Don't be a juggler who drops balls.

2   No one can avoid change today. Ten years ago Motorola
    was the world's most admired company and the market
    leader in mobile phones. Then along came Nokia and they
    became market leader. Then along came iPhone. Then
    along came Android phones. Then along came Google and
    bought the Motorola mobile phone business. Just being big
    and rich no longer guarantees success.

Ways in which the world will change (are you ready?)

We shall see increasing unpredictability in this global world.
Moscow, Beijing, Mumbai, São Paulo are as important as New
York, London, Paris, Bonn. We shall see booms and busts like
never before. Nothing is impossible … that applies to everyone.

The mighty will fall. Lehman Brothers was not an aberration,
more a sign of the times. No one is safe. Not your boss, not his
boss. No one. The 'normal' that people talk of our returning to
is over. Normal is chaos.

We live in a 24-hour society. Offices such as Google's in Zurich
are open 24/7. There will no longer be time to reflect for a few
weeks. Response times will need to get so fast that concepts such
as three-year plans are redundant. As BMW said, 'The big do
not always eat the small. The fast always eat the slow.'

brilliant tip

Be fast at work. It gives you an advantage.

Reputations will be under constant threat. No one will be able to
manage the media. Truth will out – always. Don't lie and don't
hide errors. Deal with stuff that goes wrong, quickly. Standing
still and hoping for the best is a suicidal strategy.

The brilliant marketer
of the future will have
to be agile and an
insomniac.

However, unpredictability will lead
to more opportunities previously not
considered possible. We'll need to
be master tacticians who can constantly change course. The brilliant
marketer of the future will have to be
agile and an insomniac.

The new world of marketing

It's a revolution now

We are seeing revolution in the marketing world. Media competition will hot up with more news online, more commercials,
more PR and more conversations online. So we'll have to find
new ways of reaching people.

New technology = new experiences

This will make experiential marketing far more important,
with more interactive marketing. Virtual reality will become a
reality and transform design, research and e-commerce. More
extraordinary cinematic experiences than ever will be conceived,
making this and theatre more important for marketers. The
O2 and Wembley are just the beginning when it comes to live
entertainment; we'll want to talk to people when they are having
a good time.

brilliant tip

Talk to people when they're happy and relaxed.

The shopping scene

Control of distribution will be key in the battle between retail
and suppliers. Poor service will get punished. Ethical retail

will flower – the cooperative movement, John Lewis and specialist shops – as will e-commerce. Out-of-town shopping will decline. The high street will do what Mary Portas tells it (Well, you would, wouldn't you?). We'll see more phenomena like Brighton's Lanes, Chester's Rows, Tunbridge Wells's Pantiles and Oxford's Covered Market. But moribund high streets will die. Expect to see massive change in our towns and cities. Invest in popular places because there will be losers as well as winners.

Consumer and customer relationships

The key lever will be the building of relationships between consumer and brand owner. The concept of the lifelong customer will become central to all marketing. We shall see what I call 'relationshops' – where

> The concept of the lifelong customer will become central to all marketing.

customers are treated as friends and recognised by new identification technology, so more shopping becomes a personal service experience

B2B and loyalty

In business-to-business, partnerships will be the key – with suppliers, wherever they can, going direct to customers. Death, I'm afraid, for wholesale and middlemen. Business one-to-one is the way of the future. If your people, or you, can't build relationships you are in trouble.

Winning will not be alone about money

In a world where the marketing funds seem to be running out, there are still pockets of investment that produce a powerful cut-through and situations where change is achieved through cleverness. Like taking a brand – Lucozade – which was firmly positioned in the sickroom, next to the chamber pot, and repositioning it as a healthy energy drink. Like a brand called

Innocent, which came from nowhere. Like Skoda, with its clever quality/price story – VW quality at a lower price. Like Waitrose: they price-match 1000 Tesco items and give a nicer experience. QED. Like Jamie Oliver, who's gone from a no-money kid on a Vespa (the Naked Chef) to Mr Rich today. Anything is possible.

Big challenges and issues for marketing and you

- The face of business will change. In a global economy there will be an increasing emphasis on quality and value for money, which is going to hit high-inflation China and India hard. Steiff, the soft toy manufacturer, took production back to Germany from China, saying an eye half a millimetre out turned Teddy's look of devotion into one of idiocy. It's cheaper now to make a lot of stuff in the UK than Asia.

- Corporate social responsibility is going to become more important. For example, Diageo run marketing campaigns on the need for responsible drinking – not cynically, but because not to do so is to put their relationship with government and society at risk and because they won't get young, socially responsible people to work for them unless they do. It's also the right thing to do.

- Brand partnerships will grow. Expect more and more alliances. Imagine some others: Google and Fox; Omnicom and Disney; Nestlé and Fitness First; Bose and Sony; Apple and Orange (I like that one); WHSmith and the Department of Education, and so on.

- SMEs (small and medium-sized enterprises) are going to grow rapidly. Governments regard small and medium-sized businesses as the true engine of the economy. With them there'll be a mass of new brands, and with those will come an increasing need for sharp marketing. And a whole new generation of unemployed becoming self-employed. Because of digital marketing, anything is possible now.

- Which brings me to a speculation about talent. Talent in marketing, not talent in finance, is going to be seen as key in the next decade. The brilliant marketer of the future who is very creative, fast on their feet and makes things happen is going to be very highly prized and highly rewarded.

- When companies grow, the founders have to step back and delegate, is what all the management books say. But no owner of a business should ever get rid of their role as marketing director. If you lose your touch with and love of your customers then you are in terrible trouble.

- There is a change in consumers and customers. We are seeing the increasing importance of women as the decision-makers in the home and the key influencers over all purchasing decisions. But you wouldn't think that when you see an average car dealer at work, would you?

- We are seeing the increasing importance of the 55+ sector – you know, the ones who feel about 40 and act about 30 – what American trend-watcher Faith Popcorn calls 'down-ageing'. When everyone in marketing is getting younger this potentially creates a communication problem. Go and talk to a group of older citizens and listen to what they say and what they want. Everything from bigger print to brighter light to less packaging to better manners. When you have an unsatisfied need in marketing you have a big opportunity.

> When you have an unsatisfied need in marketing you have a big opportunity.

brilliant tip

Spend an hour looking around for bad examples of marketing and decide what you would have done had you been in charge.

- In a lecture he gave to the University of Laguna in October 2008, Wally Olins said the consumer is 'answering back'. Brands, services and retailers that don't deliver are going to have an increasingly tough time. Complaints are a specific opportunity. At South Western Airlines in the USA they have a person on the board who sorts out all complaints as and when they are made. A complaint solved and a consumer placated become a friend to the company.

- The blue sky and beyond – towards the small society (not the 'big' one). Local communities are going to grow in importance and a reversal of the demolition of local shops and pubs and post offices is surely on the cards. Look at the boom in allotments. Most councils have long waiting lists. Local voices are prevailing.

- Cultural festivals are booming – Brighton, Edinburgh, Cheltenham, Hay-on-Wye, Manchester – as is the desire to play an instrument, sing in a choir (thanks to Gareth Malone and others) and to be a literary critic, hence the boom in book clubs. The arts are going to play a larger role in our lives. Are you thinking about how to take advantage of this?

- Sport is getting bigger and exciting more people. Not everyone can afford to sponsor the Olympics, premier division football, test cricket, professional rugby or tennis. But the buzz of sporting contest proves (as with live performance arts) that seeing battles in the flesh is a unique experience and a great marketing opportunity.

The future will be exciting, diverse and, most of all, unexpected, which is why the big, slow-footed corporations will have a tougher time. Even if they are very well off.

Marketing on a shoestring

If you have no money you have to think. Sometimes this means focusing on a very few consumers, perhaps a few hundred, and doing a great job for them so you have the chance of building a customer base. If you are a good decorator, maybe being the decorator everyone in one street likes and uses is a better place to be than being just another name in your county on Yell.

This is where creativity comes in. And sometimes the cleverest way of reaching potential customers is to break the mould. Take Sid our decorator. He didn't put another card through letter boxes. He got a whole load of sample paint pots and printed a message on the labels. He left the pots on people's doorsteps:

'Hi, I'm Sid. I'm a decorator. Ask me to quote if you want a job done. And I'll give you the first litre of paint I use free (even, gulp, Farrow and Ball). My phone number is ....; my email is .... Thanks for reading my pot. Sid'

Life is about choices. But what you have to spend will determine what you can afford to do.

> **brilliant** tip
>
> Doing less but doing it very well is better than spreading yourself too thin.

Marketers will have a tougher time too, especially with talking to consumers, but this means you have to build better relationships and have more straightforward and intelligent conversations. Marketing is going to be at the very core of a future that is more responsive to what people want. The winners are going to be the smart, the attentive, the curious, the energetic, the determined and the optimistic.

The core lessons of marketing history

1 **If you don't have a product** of which you are proud you're in trouble.

2 **Boring communication** won't ever work.

2 **Every marketing plan** needs to have a great idea, not just money.

3 **Learn how to talk** to consumers in their terms, not yours.

4 **Spend over 50 per cent** of your time thinking about your customers or you're getting it wrong.

5 **You have to be very fast** on your feet – marketing is a race.

CHAPTER 4

All about brands

The business of branding really deserves a book to itself. So this is just a quick overview of what a brand is and how it works. A brand is a piece of magic, a bit of 'now-you-see-it-now-you-don't' alchemy. It is not formulaic or the stuff of textbooks.

Making brands is the most exciting aspect of marketing.

Because making great brands is about building great businesses.

What is branding, what is a brand?

- Branding is the process of creating a personality for a product or service using a consistency of design and description, giving the product a distinctive feel, look and competitive position.

- A brand is something the consumer feels emotionally involved with (as though it were a person, not just a product or a service).

- A brand is something that is remembered by name.

brilliant tip

A brand is consistent and you can always trust it to deliver.

- The first brand logo was the Bass 'Red Triangle' in 1875. Wherever a significantly illiterate population saw this they knew they could rely on getting a good beer. Branding really is about putting your money where your mouth is. Once you have a brand, you let the customer down at your peril.
- Tony O'Reilly defined a great brand when he was CEO at Heinz as a product so desired that a customer would leave a supermarket if it wasn't in stock and go elsewhere for it.
- Even people who know nothing about marketing talk about brands, with the consequence that a lot of people could get very confused.

Brand ingredients

You need to be able to say 'Yes, it has these':

1 A unique name.

2 A personality – it's not just a thing.

3 A logo.

4 A designed identity.

5 A potential reputation.

6 A provenance.

7 Emotional meaning to the owner and (hopefully in time) to the customer.

8 Consistency.

9 Producer pride.

10 Availability.

11 Value greater than an unbranded product.

Brand power – what is it?

Really big brands such as Apple, Google, Coca-Cola, Samsung, Heinz, Dell, Andrex, Persil, Sony, Virgin and Canon have certain things in common: ubiquity; very high awareness and strong qualities capable of inspiring confidence, approbation and even affection. Great brands don't let you down; they are part of your life and are

> Great brands are more than just functional products.

more than just functional products. Look at what happened when Coca-Cola dared to change their recipe: proof that the brand had come to belong to the consumer, not the manufacturer.

Being part of your life lies at the heart of Action Man's ambition never to be more than feet and minutes away from a six-year-old boy. When I asked their brand manager if this meant they were thinking of Action Man toothpaste or lavatory paper, he gravely said 'Of course we are.'

People go to all this bother about branding so that they can get paid more money for their product or service than they otherwise would. The power of brands is that they make more money than commodity products or services.

brilliant tip

Study brands that you like so you can see how the company created the idea and then developed it. (For instance Coca-Cola created the image of a fat, jolly Santa Claus in a Coca-Cola red outfit in the 1930s, giving both the legend and the drink a huge boost. In other words, Coke stole, or at any rate reshaped, Christmas.)

Small brands can be sexy too

And smaller brands can have that crazy potential to grab the public imagination.

Brands such as Ben & Jerry's, the launch of which gave such a shock to the smart marketers at Diageo that they sold off Häagen-Dazs before the erosion of sales that they expected set in. Sometimes a strategic retreat is the best answer to a compelling attack.

Brands such as Innocent. A great little brand run by great people with a great attitude – their HQ in a slightly grimy part of west London is called Fruit Towers. Their web site is a joy. They come from the same stable of marketers as Ben & Jerry's, Snapple and Nike.

Brands such as Pimm's. It's the only drink that stands for something as positive as 'sunshine'. (Given which, why did they launch Winter Pimm's? That's a bit like Speedo marketing Arctic clothing or Ben & Jerry's marketing pies.)

Brands such as Peperami with its immortal advertising line 'it's a bit of an animal'. Suddenly there was a new snack hero on the block idolised by the kids – a Simpsons-type creation hit the airwaves and word of mouth took over to do the rest.

brilliant tip

Brands that work stand out because they are different and get talked about. Not getting talked about is a marketing sin.

You know you have something really exciting and sexy when word of mouth does take over, because that's when the magic multiplier of branding comes into play, when £1 of expenditure looks like £10.

The Swedish Fish story shows just this. It's a small confectionery brand that's become a bit of a cult in the USA in certain towns. It's an anti-brand – what its agency, Dial House, calls a 'bland'. A brand like Hallo Kitty or Spam that is devoid of manufactured personality and that sits there rather awkwardly. It has one flavour – 'red' – is small, anonymous, cod-shaped and is only targeted at geeks, who its creators say 'run half the world'. Do not be sneaky, smart or creative with geeks; just be. Appear only in cheap geek media and avoid advertising copy. Only use words that come from Swedish Fish fans. Spend all your money in few places. Become – thereby – a phenomenon. Here's the full story:

http://vimeo.com/17680669

Great brands tell stories

Richard French, who was chairman of the advertising agency FCO, was a proponent of whispering loudly and of being natural. Great advertising spoke consumer-speak, not Soho-speak. He felt Swedish Fish was exactly what he'd been doing 20 years ago. He was a zig/zagger to be sure. And, let's face it, if all brands were 'blands' we'd be crying out for colourfully slogan-ised, jingle-ridden brands to create competitive contrast.

'Staying neutral in marketing is tough ... great brands let the market fill a blank sheet with meaning and folklore.'

(*Alex Wibberfurth*, Brand Hijack)

Folklore is critical. Great brands are always full of stories. That's why the creation of brands always starts (or should start) with the top guys sitting round over a beer and talking

> Great brands are always full of stories.

about why they started the business and what it really means
to them.

How to create a brand – seven steps to brilliance

1 **Think about what your brand means**

It is not exactly your baby but it is very important that
you define it with the essence of your own belief and
attitudes. There need to be clear rules: 'we only use organic
ingredients; we never discount; we grow our own talent;
we have a party every six months; we give bonuses to top
performers; we respect diversity'.

> A brand without a set of principles will never be great.

It may sound esoteric but a brand
without a set of principles will
never be great. Read the story
of Will Keith Kellogg or Henry
Heinz and be amazed. Before
you do anything else, work out what this brand of yours
stands for.

2 **Find a name**

Create a name. And yes, it can be a bit silly but remember
you have to live with it. Great names have the following
components:

● **Authenticity** – Fisher-Price, Brabantia, Gunn & Moore,
Ben & Jerry's, J Walter Thompson

● **A story** – Kettle Chips, Rachel's Organic Dairy,
Speckled Hen

- **Provenance** – Thursday Cottage, Sheepdrove, Loseley, Pilsner Urquell, Melton Mowbray Pies
- **Character** – LeapFrog, Mother, Jaguar, Sweaty Betty, Mandarina Duck, Shine.

How to do it? Brainstorm. Look at your product or service. Think about it. Yes, in the end you'll create your name by thinking and thinking and one morning you'll wake up and know it. Do not spend money on getting an 'expert' to create the name unless you are a rich company.

3 **Create a logo**
Nike got that 'swoosh' for very little money from a friend. What you need is a thing to aid memory – an illustration of the idea your company stands for:

- **An artefact** – Sir Bibendum the Michelin man, the HMV dog, Johnny Walker
- **Brilliant colours** – Caran d'Ache, Google, Orange, Shell
- **A symbol** – the Hadfield's fox, the Bass Red Triangle, the [yellow tail] wallaby, the Alfa logo.

Don't get obsessed with this. It's a signature. It's a marque. If you've got it, use it. If you can't find it, don't despair. How to do it? Work with someone who can draw or is a whiz on the PC (but better to draw). Tell them what you are thinking about and see what happens.

4 **Design the brand properly**
Only now is it time for that expert to come in. You are already on the road to creating an identity. You need someone to extend, develop and refine that identity. But make sure you brief them well. And be their worst-ever client. Demand they do lots of options to open up your (and their) mind. Mark Riley who worked with me years ago did a logo design for Harriet Benton, who also worked

with me and who runs a very good catering business. Two
small businesses, one really impressive design: authentic,
strong, right. Looking at it persuaded me that professionals
are worth employing to create those clothes you'll be
wearing for a very long time.

How do you know if it's right? Trust your gut. Do not
ever settle for something that doesn't feel right. In a small
business, no one else's gut ever knows better than that of
the owner.

5 **Have an attitude that helps you find your 'voice'**
No one but you can create this. Decide exactly what it is
that makes you better, inspiring and different. Keep trying
to express it in fewer and fewer words. What is the essence
you are trying to own? Language is so tricky. Unless you
nail your tone of voice, how can you train people, as you
grow, to talk in the way you want to talk to the customers
who might buy your product.

● What does an email look like?

● What does pack copy read like?

● What's your web site like?

● What does a press release read like?

This is about style, not content, and you get it wrong at
your peril.

6 **Various faces of your brand**
Express your brand on business cards, letterheads,
envelopes, signs, posters, mugs, pencils and so on. In as
many places as, with wit (please don't overdo it), you can
make it live. Developing your web site so it reflects your
brand character is especially critical. There are a few good
designers around. But never choose anyone you don't like,
and spend time talking to them so they know what you
want.

There is one unbreakable rule: the logo, the brand name and the typeface must be constant. All of them must be always the same – always. Because that says you are consistent. That says you are remorselessly reliable. And because that's what brands are.

7 **Develop the brand personality**

Every six months, review where you are and see if you can develop your brand. Let's talk about small brands: your office decorations; staff T-shirts; Christmas cards; golf balls; pads; pencils; etc. etc. Development never stops. Have a regular 'our brand and what we can do to make it more compelling' meeting. Big brand: same thing, just bigger poster sites. Most of all see if you can get interaction with your customers. See if you can get them to respond and even to use your branded artefacts. If they like your branded mugs they may use them. Brands are 'cool' when they are well executed. Try and start up conversations. Try to become something a lot of people talk about, not just buy.

> Try to become something a lot of people talk about, not just buy.

One brand that has been brilliantly developed over time is Nike. When it had a bad year Phil Knight, founder and CEO, was not reticent in blaming, apart from other things, boring advertising and marketing.

brilliant tip

Don't ever be boring. Keep your enthusiasm.

brilliant example

Here's the Nike story, which describes brilliance in action. It borrows from a book by Robert Goldman and Stephen Papson called *Nike Culture: The Sign of the Swoosh.*

Understanding your business is key

'We got the sweaty side of health and fitness with the romance of it as well,' said Phil Knight, founder and CEO. In other words, be authentic (and simple). I love this because it's so simple and funny:

Question: 'How do I improve my times?'

Answer: 'Run faster.'

Brands depend on people

The 2004 Annual Report identified three key themes to Nike's success: 'People. People. People.' And what they believe in – their values. These values include the following, which are pretty prescriptive:

● **Rebels and outlaws** – always being the challenger (with morals), the spiky good guys

● **Not afraid to fail** – always trying

● **Not too serious** – winking at the customer

● **A bit cocky** – always walking with a bit of a swagger

● **Diversity of voice** – varying the pitch

● **Anything is possible** – there's no finishing line

● **Actions, not words** – and when words are used, only words that 'fire' actions

● **Sport is classless** – anyone can be a winner

● **Attitude beats strategy** – diversions from strategy are OK

● **Experience, not textbook marketing** – never, ever that ... please.

How to get those values

By listening. Nike spend time in the locker room, on the track, in the bar, talking, watching, changing their own minds as a result of what they hear (they are not behind their PCs). Nike is always innovating, changing, arguing; always listening for the maverick voice; always looking for what's next. Nike knows where its customers are, what they think, how they feel and where they are likely to be next.

> *'Brands like Nike tap into the basics and don't waste time on brand differentiation and stuff.'*
>
> (*Alex Wibberfurth,* Brand Hijack)

Nike has always had great, challenging ads

With great strap lines such as 'Just do it', 'I can' and 'Anyone, anywhere, anytime'.

Nike speaks to specific targets:

- **Speaking to women** – this is from Mia Hamm, US female soccer star:

  'There's a time and a place for mercy.

  And it isn't here. And it isn't now.'

- **To the racially oppressed** – Nike's first ad for Tiger Woods:

  'Hallo, world. I am the only man to win three consecutive US amateur titles.

  There are still courses in the US where I am not allowed to play because of the colour of my skin.

  Are you ready for me?'

- **To sportsmen** – to whom competition and winning are part of their DNA. This is a winning brand with the naked drive to succeed and a flick of cynical giving it street cred:

  'Winning isn't the only thing … cha, cha, cha.'

  'Also available to mortals.'

  (Viv Richards holding a cricket shoe when he was, by some way, the best cricketer in the world)

'There are two sides to a sprinter. The side that wants to crush his opponents and leave them blue and lifeless by the side of the track ... and the other, darker side.'

(Michael Johnson, 1996 Olympics)

'You can protect your eyes and your skull and your ribs and your knees and your liver and your spleen. Or you can protect your lead.'

(Wilem Defoe, champion mountain biker)

'If you're not there to win, you're a tourist.'

(Andre Agassi, Atlanta Olympics)

I love the freshness, topicality and authenticity of these. Nike gets what too few brands do – that they and their consumer are on the same side.

In praise of small brands and those who love them

Throughout this book I focus on small businesses for three reasons:

1   Most businesses are small, and my thinking here may be more useful to, or at any rate more used by, small businesses than huge ones.

2   Focusing on small businesses forces us to look at the detail that goes into marketing, rather than the big macro-thinking that goes into marketing companies such as BT.

3   Most of the best and most creative branding and marketing work is going on in small businesses right now.

> Most of the best and most creative branding is going on in small businesses right now.

This focus is not of course exclusive, because understanding how a Nike or Persil or Heinz does it matters too if we're going to understand brilliant marketing.

⚡ **brilliant** example

Quite small brands such as Cognosis, the management consultants who have a blue-chip client list, can teach us a lot. As happens so often, their aspirations to refresh and put an emphatic stamp on their brand were first manifest in their web site, where their attitudes were paraded with clarity:

'Our business is helping clients grow. Growth is what excites us, inspires us and we believe every business is a growth business.'

They have invested in coaching their 30-odd bright staff, who on average produce 12 pages of slides or reports each per day, how to 'team-plate' not just 'template' their presentations so they look as though they come from one brand, and have embarked on a 'live the brand' strategy in their offices so, without going too crazy, the Cognosis brand is omnipresent. When you enter the building you are confronted with a board of photographs of all their people. When you move around the offices words such as 'ignite', 'excite', 'inspire', 'quest', 'adventure' and 'journey' are all over – signposts to intellectual action.

One of their key achievements has been a definitive piece of research into modern businesses focusing on strategy, leadership, corporate culture and growth, called 'Edge'. A key part of their branding and marketing programme has been to make this more famous to a wider group and to promote it heavily. They are doing well: www.cognosis.co.uk

Cognosisis is 13 years old. Now, it's time (they are saying) to work on the business and build the brand values. Branding is today's big topic.

> Branding is today's big topic.

The rules of brilliant branding

1 **Brands are hugely valuable** and all the goodwill that marketing, PR, advertising and digital work creates doesn't just disappear once they've occurred, but actually accrues to and builds the brand.

2 **Beware the vandal with sandpaper** or that piece of grit; brands are delicate and damage easily.

3 **Some brands are special.** They have been created. They are consistently reliable. They mean something to the consumer beyond being a product or service. For instance, BMW is more than a car, while Vauxhall is pretty much just a car.

4 **Smaller niche or challenger brands** are increasingly beating bigger rivals through guerrilla tactics. They are often brave, cheeky and likeable. We like underdogs.

5 **Brilliant brands create buzz** and get talked about. Getting talked about and occupying brain space are not easy, but when you achieve them sales will follow, provided your product is good enough and priced right.

6 **Brilliant brands remain topical.** They live in the present, not in the past.

7 **You must have an intimate knowledge** of your product and all your competitors. Knowledge allows you to understand what your product category is really all about. If you don't really understand exactly what makes your consumers tick, you can't be brilliant.

8 **You need to build a close coterie** of brilliant people to feed your brain and imagination and inspire you. People who have years of experience working on brands. People who love brands. And people who understand that brands have DNAs and personalities, and that owning them is valuable.

9 **Understand (and respect)** the very essence and personality of what you've created. Be true to its values. Do not change it carelessly (but always ask if it's good enough and if it can be enhanced). Reinforce its strengths and regularly refresh it.

10 **Brand owners can't afford to get too cocky**, however proud of their brand they may be. Here's what Rich Teerlink, who led an historic turnaround at Harley Davidson, said:

'The day we think we've got it made, that's the day we'd better start to worry about going out of business.'

11 **Enjoy the adventure and be brave.** We do not live in easy times, but if people don't notice your brand or talk about it, you are not going to do very well. Distil your specialness and articulate it engagingly and you may be en route to creating a real, living brand. And brands really do live because they change and develop and grow. And, what's more, people enjoy them.

CHAPTER 5

All about customers, consumers and how they behave

Our end consumers are ultimately the people who matter. However well we get on with that buyer at Tesco, if the shopper doesn't like our deodorant we are in big trouble. And this applies, no less, if we are selling B2B (business-to-business) products. If the carpet tiles or computer monitors we are selling aren't up to the mark of the people who actually use them, word will get back to the market.

Yet because consumers are the elephant in the marketing room, no one mentions them enough. They are a given. And significantly they've changed. They've started to be promiscuous and try lots of different brands, they've learned how to complain and they've become a lot more sophisticated than most marketers in their air-conditioned BMWs give them credit for.

The customers are right (even when they're wrong)

Kevin Roberts, CEO of the advertising agency Saatchi & Saatchi, said he found the shift in control to the consumer was pretty scary because it meant all the marketing skills we'd learnt were out of date and that we'd have to start learning all over again.

brilliant tip

The consumer's in charge now ... keep closely in touch with what they are saying and thinking.

Here's just one example of how things have changed. Ian Wilson, who's the marketing chief at the Glasgow Science Centre, found it in an article in *Management Today*, in the autumn of 2011:

'Poor, naïve Topman has galloped turn-ups-first into a Twitter storm that's very quickly threatening to besmirch its reputation. The chain has come under fire after it produced two T-shirts that provided excuses for domestic violence and drew parallels between women and dogs. One featured the words "I'm so sorry, but" followed by a checklist of excuses including "you provoked me" and "I was drunk"; while the other features the line "Nice new girlfriend. What breed is she?" Topman seems baffled by the anger the two have elicited. "We would like to stress that these T-shirts were meant to be light-hearted and carried no serious meaning," it said irritably on Facebook.

Back in the pre-Twitter era, if someone didn't like a T-shirt, they might mutter "That's a bit much," before shrugging and buying themselves a pair of socks instead. These days, they can get online and whip their peers into a digital frenzy before you can say "mob mentality".'

Spend as much time as you can listening to as many of them as you can

> Product matters, brand matters more, but the customer's relationship with you matters most.

Product matters, brand matters more, but the customer's relationship with you matters most. We used not to think relationships in marketing mattered too much. Everything was transactional and based on sales and market share.

brilliant tip

Think about building a relationship rather than just making a sale.

Now we hear brand owners say they're interested in recruiting a customer, not in making a sale. If the relationship is a rich one and a two-way one then sales will follow, provided your product is competitive:

- **Apple** – they have great relationships with their customers. Even complaints are written in a constructive 'Please fix this, dude' kind of way, rather than being from 'Disgusted of Tunbridge Wells'. Theirs is a two-way, even-handed deal. Apple perform: their customers give them loads of feedback.

- **John Lewis** – when asked why they did so well, Charlie Mayfield, chairman and CEO, said it was down to the staff ('the partners'). The partnership is the most responsive in retail. Staff in Waitrose are empowered to sort out things off their own bat, there and then. They listen to their customers.

- **Pen-to-Paper** – It's based in Brighton. It does what it says, selling everything from wonderful cards to pens, ink, notebooks, journals. A few of us addicts of such stuff spend too much time in there. Their dream was to bring a Venetian stationer's to Brighton but the people in Brighton couldn't afford those prices. This is a British reinterpretation of Venice. And it's great. Proof that listening works.

Give them unexpected treats to say 'thank you' for being loyal – never take them for granted

Unexpected generosity pays off. We all like presents and we all feel good when we get presents:

- Nespresso sent me some delicious marzipan biscuits as a thank you for being their customer and a member of their club.

- My local garage checked over my car before I went on a

long journey – oil, water, tyres, electrics – and refused to charge me ('Don't be daft, Richard').

● Occasional free glasses of wine at a local restaurant increase the *bonhomie*, the overall wine consumption and the propensity to return.

brilliant tip

Giving surprise extras can be an incentive to buy more and to feel more positive.

Never stop wooing them and romancing your brand

Seth Godin has written at length and very well on the death of interruption marketing – those noisy TV commercials that invaded your living space. Someone said being an adman nowadays was like being an intruder entering a home, starting to talk at them (possibly telling a joke) and being vaporised mid-sentence by the remote control.

> Advertising must inform or entertain or reinforce a choice already made.

People won't take it any more. Advertising must inform or entertain or reinforce a choice already made. It's said that the heaviest users of specific car ads are those who already own or are about to own a specific marque.

We are told bookshops are dead. Extremists even say books are dead thanks to Kindle. Waterstone's (and book lovers) might disagree; the chain is now owned by a Russian oligarch and run by the man who runs the nearest thing to a literary delicatessen you'll find – Daunt Books. I spoke to some Waterstone's staff about the imminent takeover and they said:

'HMV (the previous owners) always spoke about unit sales. They never talked about books. They didn't like them. They were just another item of merchandise.'

At last they may regain some pride about their books and the stories in them. And as a book lover I want to interrupt the flow and say Kindles don't have that book smell (each one slightly different) and great bookshops, such as Daunts and Barnes and Noble in New York, are alive with a sense of exploration (especially on a Sunday).

Having pride in and passion for your brand is one part of it. Loving and continuing to love your customers is another. I never tire of the Charles Tyrwhitt or Jules Verne catalogues. I love being emailed by people who want to do business. I love the staff at Ryman's – they always seem to want to help.

Try and find out those little things in life that irritate them – and fix them

It's the little things that hurt. Pain points are the often unspoken things that really hack you off about a brand or a sector. We have a wonderful oven, a Lacanche, but two things drive me crazy about it. When working at full tilt, all ovens on and gas rings too, the control knobs are too hot to touch and the bar in front of it on which to hang oven gloves (and Lacanche oven designers) obscures the settings so you can't see if you are on gas mark 6 or 10.

Here's a better example from Fast Company, and a solution:

'Consider the humble can of house paint. For years, cans of paint have been made of tin and opened the same way: prised open with a screwdriver. But then, Dutch Boy Paint came along and introduced the Twist & Pour, an all-plastic gallon container featuring an easy twist-off lid and a neat-pour spout, which reduces the spilling and dripping typically associated with

traditional paint cans. A moulded handle allows for a more controlled pour and easier carrying.

Consumers told us the Twist & Pour paint container was a packaging innovation long overdue.'

Understand how people are different and why and how to work with this

The mass market is dead.

The mass market is dead. Two children, wife and job for life – that's all gone. There are so many variations demographically and psychographically. It is not so much about segmentation now as a fast drive towards individualism. Power lies in many hands – and it's helpful to know what they are like even at the risk of stereotyping them. Three segments are critical:

1 **Grey** – over-50s according to some seers. Get real – it's the richer over-60s who feel 20 years younger, have money, have energy and are frustrated by underusing their brains. No one has ever got marketing to this group right. The cruise ships got it most right putting 40-year-olds in grey wigs so you identified with the younger 'you' behind the wrinkles. These guys are not one cohort. In today's world we need to talk about 50s, 60s, 70s, 80s, 90s as separate groups – all customers seldom spoken to or understood by young marketers.

2 **Young** – Generations Y and Z are unlike anything we've seen before. They go from disenfranchised, uneducated, gang-member urban guerillas to independently minded graduates, with no hankering for a mortgage, stability or home. These are highly mobile project managers with advanced technological skills and great confidence. They have a vast network of good friends. They will rule the world. And that's a blessing.

3 **Technicolour** – pink, black, brown, yellow, glass-ceiling-
   breaking women and geeks. This group is leading-edge,
   style-setting and impatient about the world they live in.
   They are not homogeneous, except in the sense that
   they are driving the arts, creativity, linguistic change and
   innovation. Asia meets Africa meets the gay movement
   meets creative women meets inventive obsessives meets this
   new world. We are looking at a cauldron here and it's an
   exciting one for any marketer.

We don't want to exclude any group but it's this 'triangle of
influence' that research companies such as Penny Hunt's Red
Thread Research are focusing on right now (www.redthreadre-
search.com).

☀ brilliant tip

Two words are always a turn on – 'growth' and 'creativity'.

When you make a mistake say 'sorry' and put it right

No one's perfect but try to say 'sorry' nicely.

▶ brilliant example

From pure stupidity to a lot of purchases

My wife loves cashmere so she was cheered to discover Pure, the mail order
cashmere people, were offering a 25 per cent discount. Given the eye-
watering cost of cashmere this was a welcome piece of news. But hang on.
She was told she wasn't eligible as she was already a good customer of the
company. It was only for people who weren't 'Pure' loyalists.

I emailed them: 'My wife just called to talk about a 25 per cent discount she'd heard about to be told this only applied to "new" customers not "existing (loyal)" ones. Surely this is a mistake.'

They replied: 'Thank you for your email. Your wife has been given the correct information with regard to eligibility of the 25 per cent discount. This is an introductory discount for new customers placing their first ever order with Pure. If we can be of any further assistance please do not hesitate to contact us.'

This was not good enough so I remonstrated: 'I'm intrigued. Do you believe it's sensible to treat non-customers better than loyal ones? I think you've rather disenchanted my wife – check out how much she's spent with you.'

By now a senior officer, Trevor, was involved who started digging furiously in the hole that Pure had created for themselves:

'Unfortunately, the 25 per cent discount booklet your wife found inside a magazine is a recruitment offer that we have to run in the media to attract new business, so we're unable to use this offer for existing customers. I do realise that this may be disappointing (how about 'I'm outraged,' Trevor?), but I hope you'll understand that only by expanding the customer base will Pure be able to continue giving good prices to all customers throughout the season, like the 10 per cent discount offer we're currently offering everybody for the new collection.'

So it pays to be disloyal as a cashmere customer. And Pure seemed to think it's important for their disadvantaged loyal customers to understand their recruitment strategy.

Postscript: Purity restored

Quietly the company offered my wife all she was looking for and has been incredibly assiduous ever since. And it's cost me a lot of money in cashmere sweaters but I'm happy. Well done, Pure, but what a palaver that could have been avoided if they'd spent more time really thinking about their loyal customers.

Ask them to introduce you to their friends

The extraordinary phenomenon of social media is underpinned by its being a medium for word of mouth reaching lots of ears quickly. Never mind that corporations are now using Facebook and Twitter bogusly and potentially writing stuff like 'Hey, that Ariel is a real cool white powder. Wicked wash!' (Sorry, P&G, you wouldn't ever be so silly).

brilliant tip

What my friends think is more important than what the critics or the advertiser tells me.

A great example was the success of the independent film *My Big Fat Greek Wedding* which cost $5 million to make and was a sleeper hit. Despite a lukewarm critical reception it grossed over $380 million and was one of the top romantic comedies of the 21st century – thanks to word of mouth. For restaurants, word of mouth has always been the key. Now, with blogging, everyone has a say. I even found www.carlust.com the other day. As a brand owner there's nowhere to hide. But on the upside it's easier to get talked about now.

This is what drove the phenomenon of Swedish Fish and what constantly drives Apple's launches.

Word of mouth is the key tool in local marketing programmes and marketing within closed user groups. So when Pretzel, the UK film company, are voted the number two UK production company behind The Edge by their peers, people talk and potential buyers have a look.

Building a fan base for a group or a brand by what Keith Webb, a founder of Freedom (a music management business), described as 'grass roots ingenuity' is what makes small-marketing so interesting. His specific example was a video of a group called James Honey, comprising 70 different friends and family of the group performing different dance styles within the same track. It's charming, it's grass roots and it's ingenious. And I bet it got talked about by all the friends of that 70, so now a few thousand are stuck on Honey.

Always be faithful to your customers and their changing needs

Strangely, whilst quite a few alpha males call their customers punters, women who run or own companies have an irrational love of the people who buy or use their services. But they're right. This relationship is what will define a great consumer franchise.

> The strength of positive feelings your customers have towards you is vital to your survival.

In my FMCG (fast-moving consumer goods) infancy I was obsessed with the research company AGB, with brand-switching data and the concept of loyalists. How loyal, or better, how committed your key customers are will determine the real health of your business. When push comes to shove how many will jump ship? Whether you're selling goods or services, in FMCG or business-to-business, the strength of positive feelings your customers have towards you is vital to your survival.

> ### brilliant tip
>
> Being faithful to your customers and keeping the warmth of the relationship alive are vital.

Tide (the detergent) remains the outstanding brand leader in the USA through decades of listening, innovating and being an active partner with its customers. And, except when it dozes off or worries more about the City than its customers, Marks & Spencer does the same in the UK.

Your mission as a marketer is to ask 'how can I do more, how can I do better and how can I actually exceed their expectations and meet (or better still, anticipate) their changing needs?'

Because if you don't, someone else surely will.

Love your customers

It's that simple. And when you do and it shows, business is a lot more fun. I get the feeling I'm loved by a few places and I shop there or use them most.

The Ten Customer Commandments

1 **Remember, they are right** (even when you think they are wrong).

2 **Spend as much time as you can listening** to as many of them as possible.

3 **Give them unexpected treats** to say 'thank you' for being loyal – never take them for granted.

4 **Never stop wooing them** and romancing your brand.

5 **Try and find out those little things** in life that irritate them.

6 **Understand how people are different** and why and how to work with this.

7 **When you make a mistake say 'sorry'** and put it right.

8 **Ask them to introduce you** to their friends.

9 **Always be faithful** to them and their changing needs.

10 **Love your consumer** as though you were married to them.

PART 2

Ladies and
gentlemen:
choose your
weapons
and start
marketing

This journey around the different tools of marketing explains how they work, why they work and what to look out for if you are a buyer of them. It's meant to be as useful to non-marketers as marketers in explaining what these wizards are actually brewing in those marketing cauldrons. It's not exactly magic but it certainly smells like it. Or is it the whiff of creative gunpowder? Light the blue touch paper and stand well back.

CHAPTER 6

Madmen and the art of persuasion

Advertising is at the very soul of marketing. It is the art of persuasion, the home of branding and where the most extraordinary marketing thinking over the years has occurred. It remains the real laboratory of mind-changing communication because most people like good advertising in the same way most people like a good joke.

Smoking corsets and snappy straplines

Was it like Don Draper, Joan, Peggy and Peter when you were in advertising, I'm sometimes asked. In Britain it was much more dramatic. The language was worse, there was more violence – chairs were thrown in rage – the girls wore micro skirts, we gambled and we never stopped talking, drinking or eating. In the '60s, '70s and '80s it was a fabulous way of living. It became extraordinarily self-important. 'Labour isn't working,' said Saatchi & Saatchi's poster for the Conservative Party, and this was claimed to have won an election. It was said, when advertising was at its hip-swaggering peak, that consumers didn't drink the beer, they drank the advertising.

Is that party over?

Maurice Saatchi seemed to think so when he said in the *Financial Times* in 2006:

'Sometimes I feel as though I am standing at the graveside of a

well-loved friend called advertising. The funeral rites have been observed. The gravediggers have done their work. The mourners are assembled. Most of them are embarrassed to say they ever knew the deceased. 'Advertising?' they say. 'I'm not in that business.' At the age of 50, advertising was cut down in its prime.'

Everyone who lived through the '60s, '70s, '80s whether bankers, journalists or admen, thinks things have got worse, but the party that creates spectacular communication can never end. It thrives but with less theatrical exuberance than before.

How advertising works

Brilliant advertising seduces you and sweeps you off your feet – that's what brilliance always does. Competent advertising gives you rational and emotional reasons to consider buying a brand. But because the modern consumer is bored by most advertising, mere competence is not enough.

> Brilliant advertising seduces you and sweeps you off your feet.

Brilliant advertising, according to Martin Lindstrom in his book *Buyology*, literally lights up our caudate nucleus in the same way that nuns' caudate nuclei light up when asked to think about Jesus. Lindstrom examines brainwaves, but to those of us who spent much of our lives in advertising we can define what ingredients make the best advertising:

1 A good idea

2 Something very surprising

3 Something very funny

4 Something very memorable

5 Something very arresting

6 Something very comforting

7 Mix thoroughly and cook for about a week.

Brilliant advertising has an extreme impact and can never be ignored.

That list could go on but the key word is 'very' because brilliant advertising has an extreme impact and can never be ignored.

Is it worth the effort to aim for brilliance?

The process of trying to excel is worth the agony and angst because advertising still provides the motor-power for a lot of marketing campaigns. It's the ignition to great ideas. Even if you don't spend a fortune on placing advertisements, simply going through the discipline of thinking about how to create a stand-out piece of advertising will make you think harder and more effectively about how to sell your brand.

Recently advertising has been put under pressure by all sorts of alternative marketing, not least digital. Far fewer people watch TV so it's harder to reach mass audiences. Its role as the king activity is past in financial terms but not in influence – the advertising idea, whether presented by a meerkat or a man-man personality like Isaiah Mustafa (for Old Spice), is what any integrated campaign needs to adhere to and work.

brilliant tip

You need to see of a lot of advertising and become a student of it. The more advertisements you see, the more you will understand how they work.

How to create brilliant advertising propositions

People consume advertising in a different way nowadays. Their attention span is much shorter. They are also advertising literate – which is to say they are beginning to understand how it works – and are peculiarly resistant to hard sell.

The current need, given this short attention span, is for a phrase or even a word that describes the emotional or functional property you are seeking to own. Advertising occupies a world of very fast ideas.

brilliant tip

Advertising needs to work fast. How few words do you need? You must define a piece of territory, a particular attribute or characteristic that you want to own and around which the advertising ideas and other expressions of marketing will spin.

Listen to Bill

Possibly the greatest adman of all time was Bill Bernbach, the founder of the agency Doyle Dane Bernbach. He was very opinionated. Here's one of his opinions:

'However much we would like advertising to be a science – because life would be simpler that way – what was effective one day will not be effective the next, because it has lost the maximum impact of originality.'

Advertising, he says, is a cross between magic and art, and the key is not just the 'what' of the idea, it is also 'how' that idea is executed. So here's a brilliant tip from Bill:

'You can say the right thing about a product and nobody will listen. You've got to say it in such a way that people will feel it in their gut. Because if they don't feel it, nothing will happen.'

Advertising is about great storytelling

Advertising is the source of most great marketing communication ideas, because over time the best storytellers have very often been advertising men or women. Alan Parker, Ridley Scott, Adrian Lines, David Putnam Fay Weldon, Salman Rushdie, Wendy Perriam, and so on, all started their careers in advertising.

> Over time the best storytellers have very often been advertising men or women.

- The **'reassuringly expensive' Stella Artois** campaign depended on simple but compelling and beautifully told stories, always about the allure of the brand being too strong to resist.
- **VW advertising** has always been strong on stories. One of the most recent, featuring a small child in a Darth Vader costume discovering the force might just be with him after all, is a beautifully observed, human and funny story.

When people talk about your advertising you might be getting somewhere.

- **The US commercial for Nokia,** showing a young man using the camera on his mobile to create a visual proposal of marriage to his young lady, is like *Pretty Woman* and *Working Girl* all rolled together into one mushy story.

● **My research reveals the Lloyds campaign**, with its fantastic animation telling the fairy story of happiness in life secured by banking with Lloyds, is a success. The music, 'Wild Swans', sticks to your memory like superglue. But I much prefer Muller's 'Wonderful stuff' commercial because it's easier for yoghurt to be silly than a bank. Besides which, that's truly about what Muller can do to a grey, characterless world with its sense of *joie de vivre*. The cartoon concept has invaded their whole persona – packaging, everything – and just check out their great web site.

● **Geico.com**, the insurance company, is talked about by everyone in the States, not any specific commercial but the deluge of short parodies of the idea that there's a better way of saving money than this dumb idea … and the dumb idea story goes here. The adverts win for sheer silliness and are distant relatives of the film series *Naked Gun*.

● **The Old Spice advertising** has transformed a tired old brand that had sat on the bathroom shelf with Brut and Lynx for too long: Isaiah Mustafa, a brilliant taut script and a story of wild fantasy that ends with the great line 'Smell like a man, man.'

● **Yeo Valley** did the creative equation and turned Yeo Valley into a Yo, a west-country dairy rap brand. It's wonderful, full of appetite appeal, organic cred and fun. It's also beautifully filmed. It makes you glad to be alive, which is what great advertising can do.

● **And Berlitz**. The German coastguard, whose English not being up to much, responds to a frantic Mayday call 'Mayday, we are sinking we are sinking' with 'What are you sinking about?' It ends with Beethoven's 'Choral Symphony' and 'Improve your English. Berlitz – Language for Life'.

People take life less seriously than most businessmen. Your product will not be top of their minds. Get used to that.

● In printed media, Mastercard has unwritten stories that you have to decode. Stories about successful parents dedicating love and time to buy things for their adored children – test match ticket for son, Boyzone concert wrist bracelet for daughter. All quite 'priceless', it says, which it is when it works this well.

How to distil your story

Advertising is the art of précis and drama all in one. It has been brilliant at creating simplistic and memorable snappy straplines including these:

> Advertising is the art of précis and drama all in one.

Wonderbra – 'Hello Boys'

Heineken – 'Refreshes the parts other beers cannot reach'

Stella Artois – 'Reassuringly expensive'

Heinz – 'Beanz Meanz Heinz'

The Economist – 'How to win at board games'

Castrol – 'Liquid engineering'

'If an idea makes me laugh that's a sure sign it's a good idea.'

(Lou Centlivre, executive managing director, Foote Cone and Belding 1985)

The essential art

Advertising is a distilling process whereby we learn how to make a great sales pitch. Richard French, doyen of the trade, once said, 'I'm a professional liar: I used to work in advertising,' but he was laughing as he said it. He knew advertising was the engine of modern marketing. He also knew how to get your attention.

Despite a vast amount of work to prove how it works, advertising is an art, not a science. When he spoke about mathematics, Bertrand Russell got it spot on: 'The subject in which we never know what we are talking about nor whether what we are saying is true.' The same can certainly be said for advertising.

How to do it

This is a bit like explaining how to be a brilliant chef or brain surgeon in 100 words – it can't be done. If you can, get a pro to do it for you. The ROI will always be better. But let's shortcut on creative methodology because everyone needs to know broadly how to create good advertising to be able to judge, when presented with advertising, what good or brilliant actually looks like.

It's this simple:

1 Every ad needs an idea – just one. What's an idea? A simple unifying thought. This ad is about … one or two words. More than one idea is no good. Here's what the P (John Pearce) of agency CDP said: 'If I throw you one ball you may catch it; if I throw you two you'll probably drop both; and if I throw you three you won't catch any.' So, one ball. One idea.

2 Every creative needs to feed deeply on creativity. Just for starters, watch 100 commercials or look at 200 press ads. Watch 50 recent popular films. Spend a week watching TV, drinking beer and eating pizza. The guys good at creating

ads have been doing this for the 10,000 hours Malcolm Gladwell insists is needed to achieve mastery of anything.

3   Every ad needs a tone of voice, an attitude and a way of looking at life. It isn't an abstract thing. It's got to have a story and stories need a storyteller's voice.

Managing your agency

If your employees think you understand that brilliant advertising is worth 100 times more than good advertising they'll want to rise to the challenge.

If they think you like advertising and the way it's created they'll warm to you.

If you take them out to lunch they'll love you.

Creatives are insecure people. One of London's top copywriters said, 'I'm not as good as my last piece of work. I'm as good as my next piece of work and I don't know where that idea is going to come from.'

Trevor Beattie is one of London's most successful creative people and agency owners. He doesn't mince his words. As the creator of FCUK for French Connection, why should he? He despairs of the creative poverty that's existed for several years through lack of courage and a sense of pragmatism rather than adventure. He says something interesting about brilliance. It's better to be bad than mundane, he argues, because mundane is invisible and thus irrelevant.

Tell your agency mundane is not an option.

Thinking small

Not exactly Lloyd's Bank or Procter & Gamble are we, Mr or Ms Small Business? It's all very well talking about millions of pounds and TV but your budget is ... I'm embarrassed to mention it.

Don't be. The process of thinking in advertising, big or small, is pretty much the same. You are looking to find that magic sales pitch expressed with wit and brevity that makes people take notice.

> A great ad sometimes only has to be seen once to work.

A great ad sometimes only has to be seen once to work. How many times do you have to hear a Status Quo track to decide you liked it? Mediocrity needs repetition. Brilliance doesn't. Which is good news if you only have a small budget.

All you need is brilliance. 'Simples,' as that brilliant meerkat said. But here's the best news of all. Creative people are driven by creativity more than money. So if you are prepared to let them have their head and follow the process of 'how to do it' described above, lubricated by the occasional glass of wine, you may be pleasantly surprised.

One caveat. This is your brand, your business, your life. Do not ever go with something that your gut tells you is wrong, however smooth-selling the arguments are. It's easier to find another advertising idea than another business.

Always trust your gut.

And remember this. Whether big or small, in the current world of media choice and 'white noise', quite simply getting attention, which is the scarcest commodity there is, is your biggest problem. If that isn't a leveller, nothing is.

brilliant tip

Here's a bit of wisdom from Sam Delaney at an RSA conference on advertising: 'Advertising has too much talent to fail. It's a bit like a cockroach.'

Tell that to your creative department.

The art of persuasion

1 **Advertising is a bit theatrical,** and rightly so. It's there to dramatise brands and move people, not just tell them stuff.

2 **Brilliant communication** is rare but what we should all aspire to. Brilliant advertising transforms businesses.

3 **Advertising trades in fast ideas.** Advertising is slick and quick.

4 **Reduce your proposition** to very few words – two or three are plenty.

5 **Advertising is about the art of storytelling.**

6 **It's how you tell them,** not just the story itself.

7 **Laughter is great stuff** – make people laugh and they'll like you.

8 **Never underestimate** how hard it is to get a great simple ad.

9 **Be kind to creative people** – they are not manual workers – they are trying to pin down a jelly-like substance called creativity, which keeps escaping.

10 **Being small is not a problem;** trying to be brilliant is.

CHAPTER 7

PR – champagne, tequila and spin

I n contradiction to the flippancy of that headline, PR is the most serious business of today. In the 24/7 news world, for a business not to be able to handle the media would be derelict, careless and possibly fatal.

We are all in the image business

In the past, PR agencies seemed to be full of leggy blondes drinking Bollinger and smoking Black Sobranie cigarettes (today the very un-PCness of this is gross – who'd dare say it today ... who'd believe it appropriate ... and wouldn't it be bad PR?). But then it was all absolutely fabulous. And it still is ... fabulous. But today everyone takes the power of PR a lot more seriously. Read James Harding's *Alpha Dogs* and you'll see PR moves governments. The people in PR are generally outward going, smart and fun. But they have the steel to take on self-deluding CEOs, secretaries of state and prime ministers. Their judgement, at the level of Brunswick, Bell Pottinger, Shandwick or Finsbury, is regarded on a par with the top guys at the biggest investment banks.

The PR business still has more than its fill of beautiful people – but nowadays they also tend to have a First or 2:1 from Oxbridge, or as good as. And the sector works harder and more intelligently than it ever used to. Now it's a smart, savvy business, in tune and in touch with power, opinion formers and the 'real world'.

How PR works

PR is now at the centre of the marketing story because reputation has never been more important.

PR is about getting positive, fact-based stories about your company, its brand, its products and its people appearing in the media. But it's also about fending off and managing negative stories and potential bad press. PR is now right at the centre of the marketing story because reputation has never been more important. As the founder of JP Morgan – JP Morgan himself – said, 'Our clients' belief in our integrity is our most precious possession.' And if you think that is pompous, change clients to publics and JP to BP and you'll see nothing changes.

Today PR has to work with lightning speed and 24/7/365 media coverage. There is nowhere to hide, no time to take cover and a constant threat of an idle remark that could become the defining line in a story (As CEO in a crisis, for instance, don't lament missing your family and wishing you could regain your life.). But the PR professional should be adept at staying one step ahead of a story and recognising where it might go.

brilliant tip

For PR agency people, be obsessed with proving you give great value for money. Make the answer to the question 'What do I get for my money?' 'You get a stack of good news and avoidance of bad news.'

For in-house PR people, train your people to deal with the media so they don't blow up all your hard work with one silly remark.

PR is suddenly a lot more important

It was in the 1990s, as business got more serious and the power of PR was appreciated more and more by the politicians, that the PR world changed. It was the Alistair Campbells and Peter Mandelsons of this world who realised the importance of the next day's news story, but arguably they got too obsessed with media management, leading to a mass cynicism about what is true. In the end, PR is about solid, factual stories, not puffery. You need substance.

brilliant example

Following the takeover of Safeway, Morrisons had about as nasty a time with the analysts and business media as could be imagined. Sir Ken Morrison was pilloried as a dinosaur and the whole management and data system of the group collapsed.

Enter Mark Bolland – urbane, Dutch, ex-Heineken executive – and within a year Morrisons was (in relative terms) the UK's best-performing supermarket group with great results, a good story and something else that was magic, called 'momentum'. They even took on the OFT for untrue allegations about price fixing, won and were awarded damages. Bolland is showing a similar touch now at M&S.

PR became a professional business when its people looked at clients with a view to enhancing their clients' businesses and not just having fun. No wonder *PR Week* has suddenly become such an important magazine. PR has moved centre stage. Some PR professionals believe it is *the* critical tool as it has the ear of so many CEOs.

And 'spin'? It's nothing more than putting the best slant on what you've got. You are expected to dramatise things, of course, but don't lie. Don't ever lie. Because they won't believe you next time (which is the problem all politicians have).

But new media and the hard-to-impress opinion former have created a sense of driving downhill without brakes. Sue Wilkins of Panache PR put it like this:

'PR still has to manipulate the messages, the media and the madness ... it's exciting and the most adaptable, cost-effective, credible weapon in the marketing armoury.'

How to write a press release.

Press releases are a necessary evil, which more often than not get binned by journalists because they are boring or blatant pieces of selling. Never assume that a press release is in itself enough.

Five pieces of advice:

1   Keep them brief and always supported with good material – photographs, research, contacts.

2   Get them to the right person – better still, someone you know and are building a relationship with.

3   If possible make them an exclusive – especially if it's an interesting story.

4   See things from the journalist's viewpoint. They want to look good. Help him or her by giving them something that is new or edgy or funny or interesting. Make it look as if it's for them, not for you.

5   Local press want to fill their pages. Indulge this need by giving them great pictures and well-written material. They'll be grateful. A local slant is helpful.

Other tools of PR and how to use them

● **Telling it clearly.** The ability to create good, fact-based stories that say what the facts are, how it all happened, where and when, who did it and why and how much

impact it's all going to have.
Put in numbers. Put in facts. Be
specific.

Put in facts. Be specific.

- **Engaging attention**. Find 'hooks' or 'levers' that engage the poor, perspiring journalist you are sending this to. Something they don't know or something that adds to what they do know. Something that is unexpected ('Onions are better than Viagra' might get their attention but only if it's true). Some unexpected benefit or something that refutes previously held beliefs.

- **Instant communication**. Email is the most exciting way of spreading news fast and cheaply. E-letters can help you keep people up to date with what you are doing and be a great way of announcing things you want known. Blogs are a useful way of stating positions and starting dialogue. Your customers are at it the whole time, often reviling you. Are you responding and on the case?

- **The web**. Corporate web sites need constant updating and are usually a PR disaster – out of date and static. If you have one as a company or one yourself for your own company, update it every week. Better still, appoint a 'site-minder' who at very low cost will stop you looking sloppy and out of touch. PR is about news and your web site is a news medium. News is now, not last week.

- **TV, radio and press interviews**. Don't be caught short. You need to have the confidence, the practice and the skills to do this. Two or three messages – that's all you need to keep in your head. Plus good breathing techniques, looking the part (blue shirts on TV) and being upbeat, recognising the interviewer wants a 'good interview', not adversarial stuff, but not you doing a sales pitch either. If you try and do that you deserve to be beaten up. Anyone exposed to interviews needs training – a day with a professional coach will change your life.

Be prepared for anything. But you cannot ever be prepared for
everything.

How to use the latest PR tools

PR is now about more
than the media.

PR is now about more than the
media. Increasingly, companies are
using bespoke events to 'showcase'
their clients' activities, especially in
business-to-business (B2B) where prestigious conferences that
people see value in attending are being set up.

- **Group working breakfasts.** Where a group receives a
  short presentation, has a brief discussion and then shoots
  off to their office – getting in on time.

- **Round tables.** Where groups of people share ideas,
  expertise and knowledge. Places where breakthrough
  thinking sometimes happens. A place of debate and
  discovery when done well.

- **Workouts.** Where, a bit like town hall meetings, you
  assemble the people in the front line to meet and chew
  over how to improve a business issue. What you do with
  the outcome is the PR magic. Internal communications
  to external communications – there's something about
  engaging those in the front line that says you are honest
  about what you do. The guys who masterminded
  this technique working with General Electric, the
  massive US and global industrial and financial services
  conglomerate, are Schaffer Consulting in the USA
  (www.scafferconsulting.com).

- **Publications.** Don't be shy. If you have a great story to tell, print it, make it look important, publish (probably online or both online and in print) and be proud and be praised.

brilliant tip

Research is about facts and in PR we like hard, shiny facts.

- **Research.** Do it, use it. It's a huge tool if done well. Anyone who has a product that they believe or know has functional or remedial effectiveness needs to get third-party research to prove it, and to publish it if it works out. The media love research. And so do I, because research confers truth. There are usually too many reputations at stake for anyone to lie.

brilliant examples

Heinz running a story based on research, which got picked up by *New Scientist*, the medical press and then ran in the *Daily Mail*, among others, about the high levels of anti-carcinogenic lycopene in Heinz Organic Tomato Ketchup.

The Porsche garden at the Hampton Court Flower Festival. Normally car manufacturers park their wretched car in front of a really dull flowerbed in a really dull garden, reducing members of the RHS to a spluttering rage. Porsche demonstrated their underground, hydraulically operated garage, complete with Porsche Carrera, in a great town garden. A fun concept and it all worked brilliantly.

Orange giving tickets to the biggest gig of the year to people who donated just four hours of their time to do volunteer work. What a brilliant double whammy – what a great story.

Calvin Klein launching a fragrance called 'Secret Obsession' using actress Eva Mendes in the advertising. The commercial was a raunchy piece with an apparently naked Mendes writhing suggestively on a bed. And yes, we do see one nipple. Briefly. The commercial was banned in the USA, leading to an outraged response from the client, leading to the commercial appearing on YouTube and then being removed from that and its reappearing on other sites with a volley of blogs saying 'Show us that nipple.' It was a PR coup of massive proportions.

brilliant tip

Brilliance lies in hitting headlines. It also lies in creating momentum.

Bad PR stories

You can get salmonella in your chocolate, or the water in your bottle can have benzene in it, or your crisps can be made from decomposed potatoes, or something worse can spin out of control. Losing control of the media is like having vertigo. Very frightening, and the sort of thing that keeps you awake in the middle of the night.

When a rogue trader loses your bank billions there isn't a big enough sorry you can say or a statement that can do more than allow you to play for time. Just look as though you've regained control.

A good piece of advice for coping with disasters comes from the ex-US President Calvin Coolidge, who though terse had a great way with words:

'If you see ten troubles coming down the road, you can be sure that nine will run into the ditch before they reach you.'

▶ brilliant examples

Some PR disasters

The Galaxy problem. A nice little poster for Galaxy: which chunk of chocolate shall I have. Headline? 'Eenymeenyminymo'. No problem. Not a brilliant concept – on the OK side of workmanlike. Until it fell into the spitting pit of damnation when someone in the press noted the next line would be 'catch a nigger by his toe'.

When near facts become whole facts or suppositions become truths.

Fact: MMR jabs cause autism … no, they don't but … (there's no smoke without fire … oh yes, there is …).

Fact: plastic bags kill seabirds in their millions. No, plastic does but bags alone don't. But killer supermarket bags make a better story than industrial waste.

Fact: imported flowers cause damaging carbon emissions through being flown into the UK in big planes … er … truer fact – heated greenhouses growing flowers nearer home do far worse damage.

Brand reputation is the key measure of corporate health

The best adman became one of the best PR men – Lord Tim Bell. He understands better than most the role intelligent PR brings to bear. Here's what his company's web site says:

'In today's media-led environment, brand awareness and recall are only vague indicators of how a company's marketing is performing; brand reputation is the measure that truly matters.'

(Chime Communications)

Brilliant PR is about three things:

1　Having a strong sense of the zeitgeist surrounding a product or a market.

2　The ability to be a compelling story creator and storyteller.

3　An understanding of how to protect reputation.

The art of thinking small

In this unforgiving world there is nowhere to hide. Even if you are a small business, on a bad day you may be chased in the media by a discontented customer, or a journalist with a story to find, or a competitor who wants to have a go at you. Andy Grove, ex-CEO of Intel, said it paid to be paranoid. But let's be more positive.

Remember what we said about stories. In the 21st century the abundance of media means we can also pepper the world with good upbeat stories about your business. Because there are two qualities more powerful than paranoia and they are confidence and optimism.

brilliant tip

Sit down and see how many untold, half-told and hidden stories there are in your business.

Brilliance in PR

1　**PR ideas**

A brilliant PR idea gives the media a newsy story they can use, consumers something they enjoy and staff a level of satisfaction and fun. It's achieved by a combination of creativity (the wow factor), connectivity (knowing the right people to get the job done and talked about), hard work, motivated staff and luck (nothing in PR is guaranteed).

2 **Human qualities**
Brilliance in PR is about having a few key qualities:

● Knowing how you want to be seen.

● Having great antennae (knowing exactly where danger and opportunities lie).

● Having a nose for a good meaty story.

● Being a persistent salesperson.

● Being clear about what a story is (and what it is not).

3 **Engagement (if you're in a PR agency)**
Love your client and want to see them do incredibly well. I have never come across anyone any good in marketing services who didn't want their client and their brand to win – not for the money but because winning is what they felt they deserved. And there's nothing more exciting than a good piece in the media about your client. Imagine how their mum feels when she sees it ... and you do it by finding a good story, telling it well, relevantly and compellingly.

Brilliant PR is about being on the front foot, not waiting for something to happen.

CHAPTER 8

The 'new age' of digital marketing

Anyone over the age of 30 who expresses strong views about this medium is taking their life in their hands. The reality is the world is divided now into a series of cohorts defined more by age than culture. I love the Farmer's Boy Band rap commercial for Yeo Valley but it speaks a different language from mine. Quite simply, modern English is not the tongue of most of the population.

A friend said to me, 'You can try and understand it (and good luck) but don't try and do it. You'll die.' But there's one thing that matters.

brilliant tip

Forget the medium. Worry about how good the message is first. People buy stories, not media.

A good idea is a good idea and always was and always will be. A medium is a platform, not an idea. A digital media strategy is as tangled a piece of tautology as my saying, way back when, to a client, 'our strategy for your brand is – magazines.'

One of the saddest things I recently heard was from a young man in advertising who said 'I hate digital. At our agency they talk of nothing else and I know if I tried to talk about advertising ideas they'd think I'd lost it.'

Human needs and technology

Old world meets new world. Basic needs are introduced to new technology and we leap into a new world of communication. Of love, of friendship, of gossip, of facts, of games, of news and of photographs. For many, the thought of being away from the internet is quite depressing. But technology hasn't changed human beings, the feelings are the same – the speed of communication and the medium have changed, that's all, although racheting up the speed brings its own issues, as we shall see.

brilliant tip

When in doubt pick up the phone. When you really need to make a sale, go and meet your customer.

Because the problem is, and always has been, the human interface, or lack of it. Frank Joshi of MVine writes:

'IT has always been about transactionalising and eliminating people but you always need a human in the process.'

The need is not for better technology now but better reasons for trusting the people from whom we are buying things – the need and the biggest marketing challenge. Trust is earned, not claimed or assumed.

Welcome affordable communication

The great thing about digital is we can all do it.

The great thing about digital is we can all do it. At home. In our bedrooms. On the move. And because we are doing it ourselves we are learning at three distinct levels:

1 Dexterity of fingers and minds.

2   Stuff that we can access and didn't before know.

3   A sense of how people today are really thinking and responding to things. Doesn't ordinary TV news seem plonky now? And we only want to watch commercials on YouTube.

The key issue is that any business has a chance with digital because the cost of entry is small. Digital marketing allows the smallest to use film as a tool, which historically could only be used by big chest-thumping brands – remember the slogan 'as seen on television'. Now anyone can get their 30 seconds of fame.

Purple Cow, Blur and beyond

Stan Davis and Christopher Meyer call the speed of change in the connected economy 'Blur'. Seth Godin, author of *Purple Cow* – the seminal book on marketing, says whinging about change isn't a scalable option. The truth is nothing will ever be the same again. But the thing about this 'Digital Revolution' is it's a cultural thing as much as a technological thing and there are a number of rules we can draw from it:

1   **Do everything in real time – tomorrow is too late.** Sometimes delivering faster = worse, less thought through or plain dangerous. But in a global economy a 24/7/365 attitude is demanded as the default service by most people today.

2   **The emotions matter more than ever they did in differentiation.** Branding matters – underpinned by trust, prestige and stories. It needs constant news and buzz.

3   **The Otis Lift story – technology rules OK.** Sensors in their lifts tell Otis Control online when a lift is about to break down and what needs to be done at its next service.

Saves time and money for Otis and improves customer service.

4 **Work-life and life-life blur**. What they call 'bleisure'. Many don't stop working now in bed, on the beach, even on a horse. People want your brain, not your presence.

brilliant tip

Give more away. Knowledge is only powerful if it's shared. Be the first to pass on what you know.

5 **Create new the whole time**. We live in an 'Innovation Age'. Retailers thrive on 'new'. Everything that you do now has to be renovated, innovated or replaced the whole time.

6 **Moonlight**. Go work for your client, for a retailer, for a TV station, for a magazine, for an MP. Do new stuff. Learn. See things from different angles.

7 **Tear down your firewalls**. Confidentiality is a thing of the past. It's not what you know but what you do with it that matters. If you want to be seen as transparent (doesn't everyone?) don't hide stuff.

brilliant tip

Be big and small (at the same time). Big gives you scale and wriggle room but the best will always act small – service like a small company, with the reach and systems of a big company.

8 **Don't plan – adapt**. Old-fashioned, 'alpha male' hugely detailed three-year plans are a thing of the past. Broad, simple plans, constantly changed, are right for today.

9 **Innovation never starts with the customer**. The consumer knows what they know but seldom speculates about what's next – if you'd asked what the consumer wanted in the 1880s they'd have said a faster horse that pooed less!

10 **Churn is good**. The places to worry about are those where there's no change. People, products and ideas – change in all of them is healthy.

brilliant tip

Get attention by having something new to tell – attention is the scarcest global resource.

Understanding and using the formats

Web marketing

It's hard to imagine there not being an internet, odd to think of not having a web site and even stranger to still think of paper as the medium. If you're over 40 you may find reading on-screen hard. But the benefit of a lively or interesting web site is it defines your business and lets potential customers check you out. It also makes you work out how to present your business. It encourages you to be brave. And it makes you study the medium so you can see what else is around. My web site is www.colourfulthinkers. com, which was designed by Adam Crowley (www.bombsite. co.uk). Its creation was an interestingly interactive, to-and-fro, conversational experience – I learned a lot during it, not least that there are a lot of things hard to work out by yourself that become very easy when working with an intelligent person who listens well.

Mobile marketing

- You can set up a mobile web site by converting your PC version to the smaller format using Wordpress or 60 second Marketer.

- Establish who you are, what you do and where you are by 'claiming your business' with Foursquare or Gowalla. This gets you free listing in the equivalent of online Yellow Pages.

- Download LinkedIn to your smartphone – fiddle around and have fun. 'This is your new marketing channel,' and as with all things digital the more you play the more you'll learn. For most of us the issue is time, but spend a few hours seeing what's what.

- Run a mobile ad campaign using Google AdMob or Apple's iAd.

- Scan QR (Quick Response) codes on products or mobile web pages that have special offers. Visit BeeTagg.com to download the QR Code Reader.

Email marketing

Direct marketing by email is big news. In the USA they spend $400 million per annum on it. It featured hugely in the Obama campaign. It's easy to track and establish ROI and the benefit of email is if you don't get a fast response you probably won't get one at all. Data suggests only about 56 per cent of email messages get through and a further 28 per cent are either rejected or filtered. The further 'couldn't be bothered to read' per cent must also be quite high. But experience suggests if the message is thought-provoking enough the response rates shoot up.

If the message is thought-provoking enough the response rates shoot up.

Search engine marketing

This is the Network Rail-end of digital, all about track, efficiency, popularity and 'beating the system'. In the USA they spend $13 billion on this. It's where geeks take over (and rightly prove why they are so important). There are some key things that need doing:

1 Keyword research and analysis:

- Making sure the site can be indexed in the search engines.

- Finding the most relevant and popular key terms and phrases for the site and its products.

- Using those key phrases on the site in a way that will generate and convert traffic.

2 Web site saturation and popularity: show how many pages of the site are indexed on each search engine (saturation) and how many times the site is linked to by other sites (popularity). The more web presence you have, the easier it is for people to find your site.

3 Web analytic tools can help you to understand what is happening to your web site and measure its success. They range from simple traffic counters to more sophisticated tools that are based on page tagging (putting JavaScript or an image on a page to track actions).

But this is all quite technical and unless you are technical (in which case, hurray, and have fun) you are far better off sitting down with an expert and being told how much it will cost to transform your site from just being there to being 'active'.

Data mining

The most exciting thing about this technology is we can begin to play with customer data in a way never before possible. We can not only see where, when, how often and how much people buy,

> We can begin to play with customer data in a way never before possible.

we can track how their buying patterns change, we can see how they correlate to external factors such as weather, advertising and sales drives. We can also establish who they are linked to and who they are influenced by. We can actually do that thing that Peter Sarstedt sang about in 'Where do you go to, my lovely?':

'Tell me the thoughts that surround you,

I want to look inside your head.'

Any marketer worth his salt will find this amazing. Big ideas are great but the engineering of consumer behaviour is the stuff that really turns us on. We are all geeks at heart.

Apps and all that

Application software can either be bundled as a portfolio of software applications that come with Windows, for instance, or be individually available as what are mildly described as 'killer apps'. Here are the seven best practical ones according to *Tech Crunch* in 2011 – their words, not mine:

1 **Slacker Radio** A fantastic alternative to Pandora, which carries a larger catalog and offers Premium accounts that offer something we've always loathed about Pandora – unlimited song skips. (Similar: *Pandora, WunderRadio, Last.fm*) http://www.youtube.com/v/ lPFdmjR30kM&hl=en&fs=1&

2 **Hey Where Are You** A beautifully simple application that takes advantage of Push Notification, by letting users ask and answer the question 'Hey, Where Are You?'. (Similar: *Loopt*)

3 **Textfree Unlimited** Currently the best alternative to high

SMS plan costs, offering free text messaging using Push Notification.
http://www.youtube.com/v/S4hiEGo9Hv4&color1=0xb1b1b 1&color2=0xcfcfcf&hl=en&feature=player_embedded&fs=1

4 **Bento** Create simple databases to store information about every aspect of your life.

5 **TweetDeck** Our new, favorite Twitter client that takes advantage of the same layout as its desktop counterpart – multiple columns, separation of user groups, and more. (Similar: Tweetie, Twinkle, TwitterFON)

6 **Print and Share** Print files, emails, web pages, contacts, images and even snapshots direct from your camera, straight to your home printer. Simple setup and works perfectly.

7 **Flight Tracker** Watch flights in real time and get up-to-the-minute arrival and departure times. This has saved me countless delayed pick-ups from the airport.

The role of iPad

The legacy Steve Jobs leaves is a very big one. But until he fixed the concept of a tablet (which Apple didn't invent) there were laptops, notebooks, increasingly smart phones and PCs. The iPad has transformed business as well as being a wonder toy. It's portable, book-sized, has amazing graphics and a huge memory. So many people just like it (simply like it) so much that it's invaded places normally controlled by the IT Department. Like board rooms. Like departments. Like universities. Like executives on the move who had, until recently, not understood how virtual working could be.

A technosceptic was introduced to it on a train journey and shown the painting app 'Brushes'. After a few minutes of silent trial she asked 'How much is this thing?' That is what I think is called a 'buying signal'.

Well, small business, what do you think?

Research amongst American SMEs recently showed 43 per cent didn't think social media were necessary to their business – a big 'no' – whilst only 12 per cent said they were a must – a small 'yes'.But I bet this is changing as I write.

Word of month is regarded as by far and away the most important marketing tool. Advertising and PR are not seen as very important at all.

This only goes to show the terrible job agencies have done at helping good small businesses work on their marketing strategies. And how slow people have been to realise that digital marketing is all about creating word of mouth very efficiently.

brilliant tip

Digital lets you try things out – fast and cheaply.

The lovely thing about digital is nothing gets written in stone.

The lovely thing about digital is nothing gets written in stone (sorry, Moses) – you can try new things and you can change track. But remember one thing. A bad idea is a bad idea. A good idea is a good idea. And people usually respond to good ideas.

Digital makes us all the same size (except smaller is better)

For the first time in my life literally anyone can start a business, can create a brand or can actually bring a dream to life for virtually no money.

Digital means you can think differently and faster. You look bigger but you think about detail. You are in control of your vision and are not being ruled by a bureaucratic monster.

Suddenly anything is possible:

1   Imagine launching your brilliant British pie business without digital to help.
    Imagine not having to get supermarket distribution.
    Imagine making pies fresh to order and delivering them the same day.
    Imagine the story you have to tell.

2   Imagine launching your own PR company by giving online advice.
    Imagine writing up some great case studies.
    Imagine being positioned as a source of great information.
    Imagine no one knowing you are launching this business from your bedroom.

3   Imagine creating your own florist online.
    Imagine how brilliantly colourful your site would be.
    Imagine the benefit of carrying little stock until you've worked out how to run the business.
    Imagine focusing on what you are brilliant at – arranging flowers.
    Imagine turning your old car into a brilliantly decorated flower-mobile – checking out young artists on the web who can do it for you.

CHAPTER 9

Social networking – is this the future of marketing?

Robert Scobie, who's a tech journalist, reviewed Twitter, Facebook and Google+, comparing their virtues, and concluded he couldn't live without all three and that this meant he needed three monster screens side-by-side. Social media are changing lives, filling time, increasing conversation intensity and making a difference.

We need to be loved and reaffirmed

Social media, reflected Scott Leonard, the ex-360 brand director from Ogilvie and Mather, are the counters to the 'unsocial media' that interrupted our lives for half of the 20th century. Look at a film on any commercial channel and agree how desperately irritating advertising breaks really are.

brilliant tip

Social media serve primal needs to be connected, to show off, to gossip and to be affirmed in importance. Understand the need that each element serves.

The need to be loved has been served by social networks – Facebook feeds our need to connect, Twitter our need to show off to our friends and

> The need to be loved has been served by social networks.

share news, Google+ our need to know, and LinkedIn who we are and what we've done and achieved. In a world without boundaries, social media provide the online social clubs a younger generation needs and do so with brilliance. Most comforting of all, there is a gather-round-that-campfire feel about them, which in a comforting way takes us back to the oral storytelling days of *Beowulf*. As Ed McCabe, legendary adman, said: 'There's nothing new under the sun, just a better way.'

The innovation of social media is a better way.

The social media landscape

Frank Joshi, founder of MVine and Knowledge Peers, observed that consumers were always three to five years ahead of corporates. So what is happening today on social media is an indicator of the marketing future.

- **Facebook** With a claimed 800 million users, Facebook is huge, but try selling in an old-fashioned way on Facebook and you may get killed. As a way of starting a conversation about your product or brand it may be useful. Just be aware you are on your own and then the global public takes over. Market on Facebook and you may lose control. But chances are nearly everyone you know is going to be there.

> Chances are nearly everyone you know is going to be there.

- **Google+** Traffic to Google+ spiked 1,200 per cent in the first few days following its public launch in September 2011, but then plummeted by 60 per cent, according to a report from a data analytics company, Chitika. Google+ hit 25 million unique visitors in its first month of operation, making it one of the fastest-growing social networks of all time. But the most recent unofficial count pegged the number of Google+ users at 43 million. Google+ may not be convincing new users to stick around … time will tell. It has a more magazine feel to it – comments are longer and more thoughtful than newsy Twitter. Search is unsurprisingly good. Photos and videos are very good.

● **Twitter** With 100 million users Twitter is not much used by the very young but is the medium of choice for opinion-formers, businesses and celebrities. Its 140-character limit makes it easy to work and assimilate. It is the place to get the news first. David Cameron uses it (whilst Barack Obama has just embraced Four Square). The best advice I had on Twitter was from singer-songwriter Emily Baker, who described a late-night conversation about musical preferences with a group of knowledgeable insomniacs that led to a DJ playing her music. She said, 'I could have asked him – that would have been too crass – but we were having an interesting conversation and it happened.' Lesson: be interesting and things happen. Twitter has news of global brands (http://twitter.com/#!/scoblemedia/world-news-brands) – that's useful.

● **LinkedIn** This is the world's biggest business network with 100 million members. Kevin Eyres, its European MD, describes it as 'one of the most exciting companies in the world' to new employees, which sounds terrific and inspiring. It's necessary to be on LinkedIn if you are serious about keeping in touch with old colleagues and it has useful groups you can link into and news on marketing issues.

Things are moving very fast

In the UK in 2010 Google was the second most influential brand, Facebook the fifth, Microsoft sixth and Twitter the tenth so the story is one of mighty, powerful brands fighting and scrambling for control.

The story is one of mighty, powerful brands fighting and scrambling for control.

brilliant tip

Speed is the key. Our world, opinions about it and trends all develop in a blink. Get used to using the topicality of the social conversation.

When people like me start to take an interest in social media, maybe it's time to move on. And move on is what a lot of people are doing. Growth has slowed in the past 12 months and in the USA all but stopped amongst 16–24-year-olds. Amongst the under-30s university-educated the decline is pronounced and this is a new trend. Activities that are all showing double-digit decline are messaging to friends, sending presents, joining groups and searching for new contacts (Source: GlobalWebIndex).

The word from many is that leaving Facebook, which has absorbed so much of their life and time with people who are not really friends but casual hangers-on, is incredibly liberating. But this brand is still phenomenal, even if it is showing signs of flat-lining into maturity with people spending time on what they want and experimenting with less zeal. The generational differences are interesting and Daryll Scott, creative director of Noggin, is very clear of the dangers commentators like us face:

'For us who are a little older, we can engage in this medium but it's not natural or effortless, it costs us energy so we don't do it with the adequate level of frequency and immediacy – so as activity swells, we are not "on it" enough to capitalise on it so the fuse splutters out. We are Eddie the Eagle, we are getting in the game with boundless enthusiasm but we don't stand a chance.'

What are social media and why should you use them?

I am indebted to Emily Conradi for what follows, which is an idiot's guide to social media and as such very useful.

Facebook

What is it?

http://www.facebook.com – the number-one social network.

How do companies use it?

Encouraging loyalty by getting people to become a fan or to 'like' you ('like-ing' will appear temporarily on a person's newsfeed), exploring new demographics, expanding brand image, incorporating other media campaigns, competitions and promotions.

There is A LOT of stuff online about using Facebook for business. More information: http://www.techipedia.com/2010/how-to-use-facebook-for-business-and-marketing/

How could you use it?

● Have a look at this guide: http://www.facebook-studio.com/fbassets/media/856/FacebookBestPracticeGuide.pdf

● Create a fan page: https://www.facebook.com/pages/create.php

● The most used aspect of Facebook is uploading photos so perhaps you should make use of images.

● You could use it to encourage dialogue about your market sector, e.g. get people to vote on their preferred product.

● Drawbacks: Would you be engaging the right audience? Are the demographics right? Do you have time to engage?

Examples:

http://www.socialmediaexaminer.com/top-10-facebook-pages/

http://www.socialmediaexaminer.com/
top-10-small-business-facebook-pages-2011-winners/

LinkedIn

What is it?

http://www.linkedin.com – social network for professionals.

How do people use it?

To increase visibility and self-promotion, find useful individuals/
groups, start/join discussions, gather feedback/opinions/advice,
and up-to-date information about what is going on out there (http://
gigaom.com/collaboration/33-ways-to-use-linkedin-for-business/

http://www.interviewmantra.net/2010/03/what-linkedin-is-for.
html).

How could you use it?
* Get referrals for your work.
* Build your networks for promotion and recruitment (and
  the other reasons mentioned above).

Examples

http://www.mpdailyfix.com/
how-i-was-wrong-about-linkedin-with-2-mini-case-studies/

http://www.youtube.com/watch?v=W4nD6y-PnUY

Google+

What is it?

https://plus.google.com/ – a new social network by Google.

How do people use it?
Create a profile and collect +1s (similar to 'like' in Facebook or referrals in LinkedIn).

Not ready for business yet: http://www.socialmedialogue.com/ google-plus-for-business-pages-to-launch-later-this-year/654/

How could you use it?
Would be fantastic for integration with web sites, Google Maps, analytics and adwords, etc. Useful for SEO too.

Examples
Not much out there yet.

Twitter

What is it?
http://twitter.com/ – microblogging site, second only to Facebook in popularity. It consists of short, bite-size updates in real time where you can 'follow' those that tweet, and anyone with an interest can also follow you.

How do others use it?
- Create hype, raise awareness and follow progress within the community of interest (http://business.twitter.com/)
- Tweets can be targeted to certain people or events using a #, so as well as following individual people you can also follow conversations. You can also 'retweet' other tweets you find interesting.
- This is useful: http://www.chrisbrogan. com/50-ideas-on-using-twitter-for-business/

How could you use it?
- Useful to follow interesting people/companies/marketing news and likewise keep people informed.
- The use/benefits are similar to a blog, but just bite-sized

and easier to digest and more accessible (e.g. you can tweet from your iphone, on the go).

Examples

http://www.nytimes.com/2009/07/23/business/smallbusiness/23twitter.html

Blogs

What is it?

Here is an explanation: http://youtu.be/NN2I1pWXjXI

A formal definition is: a web site on which an individual or group of users record opinions, information, etc. on a regular basis.

How do others use it?

● To keep their network informed and engaged with current information, future plans, etc.

● To share and reflect on experiences.

● To promote expertise and knowledge.

● To make connections in related fields.

How could you use it?

● You can give your own views and highlight other expert advice in your field from sites/blogs/papers you read.

● Answer your most frequently asked questions, point to leading people (and get them to link to you), put a voice behind your company, encourage (and respond to) comments.

● You can create a blog through moonfruit – 123 Ranking could advise what's best for SEO.

Examples

http://mashable.com/2011/03/30/small-business-blogs/ (with some additional blogs of interest in the comments section).

YouTube

What is it?

http://www.youtube.com – allows users to discover, watch and share videos.

How do others use it?

Advertising, viral campaigns, training, 'how to' videos, filming events. Basically anything that involves promotion. YouTube videos are very easy to share, embed and spread, and some people will often choose to watch a two-minute video rather than read a page of text.

http://www.businessinsider.com/youtube-business-2010-2# why-should-you-use-online-video-1

How could you use it?

- Interviews with people about communications and presentations. 'How to' examples.

- You can have your own dedicated YouTube channel that you can brand nicely, or just post on the main site. You can also control the levels of access for your videos, e.g. you can use it to host videos you've made but restrict access so people can't find or access them without the url.

Examples

http://blog.socialmaximizer.com/youtube-business-use-cases/

Flickr

What is it?

http://www.flickr.com/ – an online photo management and sharing application.

How do people use it?

It's actually against Flickr's terms to use it for business, but companies still set up profiles and use images to promote and spread what they do. The following link is a very exhaustive list of how it can be used for business:

http://b2bformula.com/2010/04/29/44-ways-b2b-companies-can-use-flickr/

How could you use it?

Share images that are interesting. You could also use it as a forum to discuss good marketing principles.

Slideshare

What is it?

http://www.slideshare.net/ – the world's largest community for sharing presentations.

How do people use it?

● http://www.slideshare.net/rashmi/slide-share-business-final

● This is helpful as well: http://www.planetcontent.co.uk/slideshare-content-marketing-strategy

How could you use it?

● By putting on a great presentation about the sort of stuff you do, so long as don't try and 'hard sell'. Establish the sort of person or people you are.

Examples

Type in any key word you can think of to their search bar to see the sorts of things that come up.

Other case studies

● http://techcrunch.com/2010/07/17/how-social-media-drives-new-business-six-case-studies/

● http://www.interactiveinsightsgroup.com/blog1/social-media-case-studies/

● http://mashable.com/2009/02/06/social-media-smartest-brands/

Other social media sites that might be relevant

- **Delicious** formerly **del.icio.us** (http://del.icio.us/): **social bookmarking** site for storing, sharing and discovering web bookmarks.

- **Digg** (http://digg.com/): a community-led way to find and share news online.

- **Ecademy** (http://www.ecademy.com/): as described by them – a business networking for the digital age. Ecademy is a membership organisation for entrepreneurs and business owners who belong to a community that connects, supports and transacts with one another. It aims to help small to medium businesses quickly and effectively find the right kind of people they need in order to grow.

- **Knowledge Peers** (www.knowledgepeers.com): peer-to-peer learning communities on issues that trouble all executives. Useful because you can talk to and hear people in your own markets.

- **Netlog**: (http://en.netlog.com/): a social network that specifically targets young people in Europe.

- **StumbleUpon** (http://www.stumbleupon.com/): good for SEO optimisation. A social networking site that focuses on allowing you to share, 'like' and rank content online, and helps you find more of the sorts of things you like. For a video explanation go to: http://www.stumbleupon.com/productdemo/

- **Tumblr** (https://www.tumblr.com/): a popular site that allows users to set up their own blog that links up to other social media very easily.

- **Xing** (http://www.xing.com/): another professional business network.

- **Yelp** (http://www.yelp.com): a social bookmarking site that describes itself as an online urban city guide that helps people find cool places to eat, shop, drink, relax and play, based on the informed opinions of a vibrant and active community of locals in the know.

'It ain't what you do, it's the way that you do it ...'

And the old Sy Oliver and 'Trummy' Young calypso then goes on 'and that's what brings results ...'

The good news is that using social media is mostly to do with common sense, a touch of human sensitivity, persistence and the way that you do it. Yet most brands use Twitter accounts as business updates. There's no conversation, no attempt at relationship-building. It's just another post–traditional-one-way style of thinking.

brilliant tip

Be loose and conversational in the two-way world of social media. Take off your marketing presentation hat.

Brands have to be careful on social media. Don't broadcast, don't hector, but do be quietly conversational. Logos come last, niceties come first. People matter more than brands in conversation. Some businesses often forget why they're even online. Often it's because their competitors are or because they've been told that anyone without a social-media strategy is doing the marketing equivalent of wearing drainpipe trousers. If there is no clear link to your business aims then it's a waste of time and money. As so often in life, this is more about how you do things rather than what you do. And there's one other thing that is very human about social media. They're spontaneous. They're fast and they're now. They shouldn't be overly crafted.

Revolution and authority

What happened in Tahrir Square in Cairo, in Tripoli, in Edmonton and in Liberty Square NYC was helped, given momentum and shaped by social media.

This communist joke is an example of how the red ink of instant communication has changed our societies and the potential of our world:

> Instant communication has changed our societies and the potential of our world.

'A guy was sent from East Germany to work in Siberia. He knew his mail would be read by censors. So he told his friends: "Let's establish a code. If the letter you get from me is written in blue ink it is true what I said. If it is written in red ink, it is false." After a month his friends get a first letter. Everything is in blue. It says, this letter: "Everything is wonderful here. Stores are full of good food. Movie theatres show good films from the West. Apartments are large and luxurious. The only thing you cannot buy is red ink."'

Have you got a spare hour a day?

The hollow laugh says everything … of course you haven't. But you can't embark on a social media programme without being engaged.

As a small business these sites represent your best, virtually free way of building awareness of the sort of business you are, the sort of person you are and interesting things you've discovered. They allow you to have casual conversations with the sort of people you really want to meet. It is not a medium for elevator pitches; it is a medium for showing you are a person worth listening to.

But the sites are only virtually free. Because they will take your time. To be on the map with the new market of consumers you have little choice but to be involved. And chances are you'll begin to find you enjoy it. Just don't suppose nothing else matters now. It's a medium, not the message in its own right.

Key points to consider

1 **Linking up these tools as part of a larger strategy.** Most of these platforms have widgets that make it easy to set up linking across various platforms – i.e. when you submit a new blog post it can automatically be fed to your Twitter/Facebook newsfeeds. Make sure you link everything to/from your web site and keep brand identity the same. You can also use various services to stay on top of what is published by the people/organisations you are interested in following, e.g. through the use of RSS feeds.

2 **Stay focused**. There are a lot of interesting tools and 1001 ways to deliver information. Always try to bear in mind whom you are trying to target and what you hope to achieve.

3 **Engagement**. There is no real value in using any of these tools if you don't have the time to properly engage with them. Social networking needs to be two-way. If you just want to put up information and that's it – that is what a web site is for. You need to engage with users or you won't get anything out of it (imagine it like a conversation). For further tips on this go to: http://www.techipedia.com/2011/social-media-dating/

4 **How will you assess value?** You may want to consider what ROI you will use to track the success of various social media initiatives.

5 **Identity management**. Who are you? The person behind the company often makes it a more personalised and less formal interaction, but you need to be mindful of the other information on your profile and whether you want

this shared or to represent your brand (e.g. the photos you already have on Flickr).

6 **Lurking.** You can set up profiles to most of these tools and don't have to actually use them until you are ready. It's a good way to gain familiarity, understand the options and see what others are doing with the tools before you come up with your final social-networking strategy.

CHAPTER 10

Sponsorship – getting your name up in lights

There's something very appealing about sponsorship, just as there's something deeply enjoyable about sport, film and fame. It feeds our vanity to rub shoulders with the successful, especially if somehow or another you get to feel you 'own' a bit of them. What follows warns you about letting the heart overrule the head. Sponsorship is a marketing tool that must be handled with circumspection and professionalism.

> Sponsorship is a marketing tool that must be handled with circumspection and professionalism.

How sponsorship works

Money. You pay money to own (or co-own) the rights to a player, car, horse, event, series or whatever. You can sponsor almost anything. When you get sponsorship right it can work incredibly well for you. You get the association of being linked to a winner and, if you are lucky, you may have a wonderful brand ambassador. Or you can waste a lot of money ... Well, which is it?

brilliant tip

Expect to double the cost of sponsorship rights on marketing them. Exploit your sponsorship fully or don't do it at all.

Why sponsorship is growing so fast

Sponsorship, the pundits said, was economy-dependent, more likely to be used in the good times. Yet in the USA between 2009 and 2011 expenditure will have actually grown from $16.5 billion to an expected $18 billion, whilst global expenditure grew 5 per cent to just under $50 billion in 2010 and was expected to grow again in 2011 to a level just under 10 per cent of the value of global advertising. So sponsorship is big business.

What's driving sponsorship against the odds is the money being poured into sport (especially by the 'super-rich', the allure of the really big events, the Olympics, World Cup, World Series and the Golf Majors), the overall growth of global sports (sports coverage on the media), and the excitement sponsorship can bring to leaders, staff, customers and consumers alike.

At the top end of sport, investment will increase, coverage and technology will get cleverer and sponsorship will follow.

At the lower-cost end of things the sun is also shining

Not all sponsorship is hugely expensive – especially if it's local or niche. Sometimes putting money into, say, a local golf event or a golfer to entertain your golf-loving customers can pay dividends. Getting to spend hours of quality time with important customers is a really sensible investment if you do it with style and a sense of passion. So, too, may an investment in a cause-related event motivate young talent in your business or younger customers who are concerned about certain issues.

> Your ultimate aim is to sell more of your product at the lowest possible cost.

Avoid controversy. Avoid people who are on a mission to convert. Your ultimate aim is to sell more of your product at the lowest possible cost, not to be an altruist and put your company's money to charitable ends. Always think about what you want to achieve.

⚡ brilliant tip

Aim to build better relationships and understanding with your customers.

But if you are going to sponsor a charity, check them out through the Charity Commission, speak to other sponsors and insist on meeting the CEO and chair of trustees. Judge whether they could speak convincingly and amusingly to your key customers. Study their accounts. Judge how important you'd be to them.

▶ brilliant example

Journalist Kenneth Hein claimed Red Bull was Austria's biggest export since Arnold Schwarzenegger. It's bigger, Kenneth, much bigger and touching more lives. The brand sells over three billion cans a year and, substantially through sponsorship, has woven its way into the life of the young and the daring. No one has ever owned so much high-energy sport.

From BMX ('The Red Bull Fighters') to air races, windsurfing, snowboarding, breakdancing and cliff diving, record-setting Red Bull has stood for success and for adrenalin. Its slogan 'Red Bull gives you wings' gives it bragging rights in any sport where speed counts. It's even in a video game, 'Worms 3D', where drinking Red Bull gives the worms the ability to move faster.

As in its distribution strategy, where it's preferred to own dedicated, new, young distribution set-ups rather than multi-franchised professional outfits, Red Bull has used sponsorship in a uniquely aggressive way to build its presence with the people most likely to buy into the values of the brand and to get the notice of a wider audience.

Now a huge global brand, it's spread those Red Bull wings and was again in 2011 the huge success in Formula One, with Vettel and Weber. The advertising value-equivalent they get from Formula One was estimated at £220 million in 2010, when it received almost a quarter of the total received by all the teams. Red Bull Racing is wholly owned by the drinks company and made a £2.8 million pre-tax profit in 2010, with 75 per cent of this down to F1 and other projects contributing the remainder. Not too many companies make so big an ROI from their marketing spend. I wish Red Bull were running the global economy.

brilliant tip

Red Bull teaches us how to do sponsorship with energy and conviction.

Study their smaller sponsorships such as breakdancing, to see how they get the fan base to be the sales force, and how building communities that spread their wings under the auspices of Red Bull works so well. Their success is about being smart, not being rich.

This is another fine mess you've got me into

The trouble is too many sponsorship decisions are made rather informally at chairman or CEO level, leaving the poor marketing people to sweep up the debris of a glamorous dinner party conversation that led to a good-idea-at-the-time investment decision, but is simply not thought through. If this has happened you have little choice but to make the best of it and, whatever you do, try to ensure you merchandise the sponsorship as brilliantly as you can. Do the following:

1 Make it look as though it is thought through

('post-rationalisation' is the most valuable marketing tool a company can have).

2   Make sure the sponsored body becomes very visible to staff and their families; aim to grow a huge grassroots 'sales force'.

3   Make it seem involving to all your major stakeholders – suppliers, customers and local media – never underestimate how much you can get out of them by treating them as important partners in the enterprise.

☀ brilliant tip

Warm up your key opinion-makers; don't embark on a sponsorship and then neglect it or starve it of funds.

▶ brilliant example

Learn the lessons from others:

● Brighton and Hove Albion's main sponsor, (impressively) binding club and community in close embrace, is BrightonandHoveJobs.com.

● Barclays Cycle Hire is an enormous success in London, now with 6000 bikes and 400 docking stations and more than 4 million journeys or so to date. It costs £5 million a year for a five-year period (just under 20 per cent of the total cost). The bikes look great, they're everywhere and the concept is going to fully fund its annual cost. London is happy, bikers look very happy, Barclays should be ecstatic.

● However, sometimes things go wrong. The Tiger Woods saga was a sad story of sponsors walking away as his personal soap opera unfolded. Gillette, Gatorade, Accenture, AT&T, Golf Digest and Tag Heuer all deserted him; Nike and EA Sports stuck by him. I rather preferred them for putting loyalty first. I suspect (and hope) they will come out the winners.

▶ **brilliant** example

It was Karen Earl, chair of the European Sponsorship Association, who said:
'Sport is extremely engaging and it can give a human face to industry.'

No more so than in rugby, where Brains Beer renewed their sponsorship
with the Welsh Rugby Union team. So far so good, but it's rendered
brilliant for all concerned by the very close support and participation
the team gets from Katherine Jenkins and Charlotte Church. They are a
brilliant, sexy duo – very Welsh and very enthusiastic.

Branded entertainment

Branded entertainment is sponsored TV or film. Soap operas
were originally called that because they were sponsored by
Procter & Gamble, makers of – soap.
This world is being reinvented with
new focus. Sir Martin Sorrell for
one, and his is the loudest voice
in marketing services, believes that
sponsoring films and TV series is
going to be the next big thing. The buzz phrases are 'content
partnership' and 'entertainment brands'. Think about what
Disney did by turning a theme park ride into a global brand with
Pirates of the Caribbean.

> Sponsoring films and TV
> series is going to be the
> next big thing.

★ **brilliant** tip

'The age of using adverts as a megaphone to yell at people and
irritate them is coming to an end. If you are smart and have a
message to get across you have to do it in a way that's agreeable,
sensitive and welcome.'

(Ed Warren, a creative executive at Mother Advertising Agency)

This is not product placement

Product placement used to get bad press, as it seemed to be overdone and overt in James Bond films and *Coronation Street*. Ofcom seemed to turn a blind eye. But branded entertainment is something more exciting. Think of your 'brand' as the 'executive producer'. Think of the next local pantomime written with your brand in mind. Imagine Cinderella being sponsored by a shoe brand. Timberland brings you Cinderella in 'the shoe that really fits'.

They're already at it in droves

It started in 2001 with BMW Films doing *The Hire*, a series of acclaimed shorts. Now all the big names are getting in on this: Coca-Cola's 'Stepping Stones' programme for people with learning difficulties on NBC; P&G on the American version of *The Apprentice*; and Amex, Budweiser, Toyota and Ford are all in there. In the UK we have the *Nokia Green Room* – a music TV show on Channel 4.

Fay Weldon wrote a novel, *The Bulgari Connection*; *Somers Town* was an award-winning film into which Eurostar pumped £500,000; and *Pot Noodle: The Musical*, featuring events from their commercials, appeared at the Edinburgh Fringe.

The problem is selling to the smart consumers of today

'Advertisers are realising that if they create their own content they don't need to pay for ad space, they have greater control over how their brand is portrayed and ideally they create a more in-depth and involving interaction between consumer and brand.'

(Nick Chapman, brand strategy director at Venables, Bell and Partners in San Francisco)

But there's a problem:

'Brands tend to want to be shiny and positive, while people generally prefer entertainment about complicated people doing stupid or dirty things to each other.' (Nick Chapman again).

brilliant tip

Today's marketing work needs to be authentic and edgy. Bland is dire.

This is new territory. In the future, advertising agencies are going to work with producers on content, making brands the new patrons of great movies and shows. It's going to mean that money to do great work will be available.

In the brilliant world of marketing we are going to create 'brand architects' who will spend their time working out precisely what their brand is and what their brand is not and how the perfect fit with a film, series, play or TV event can be constructed. And, unlike in the past, the associations are going to be subtle and interwoven, not crude. The issues are going to be understanding exactly what emotional territory you want to occupy and how available it can be made. This won't mean a lot to an average marketer at the moment, except (being an intelligent marketer) they should be speculating what it could mean. So watch this space and imagine *Guinness: The Epic in Black*, *The Samsung Opera* and so on.

brilliant tip

Big brands need big ideas. This area is one of innovation ... and courage is needed.

All brands need affordable ideas too. Any brilliant marketer is going to track what the big brands are doing here and see what works. I can't wait to see the 'Orvis Fishing' programme or the 'Callaway Golf Heroes'.

When brands help create best sellers it's time to watch out. The acid test will be when a big brand helps create a top-rating TV series. Then we'll see Hollywood and Wall Street get very, very friendly with each other. When a Heinz gets credited with inventing the next *Simpsons* the world will have moved on.

> The acid test will be when a big brand helps create a top-rating TV series.

Thinking carefully and thinking small

Sponsorship can sometimes be a surprisingly good-value activity if, in a B2B situation, whatever it is that you sponsor allows you to entertain customers and their wives well.

One basic rule will always apply. Can you make it look fresh, creative and strongly branded? Can you own it?

An ad in a theatre programme seems almost always a waste of time. However, ownership of one performance, with you standing up at the beginning and saying who you are and why you're backing it, may be a great deal. Just don't be sold because you feel sorry for the swimmer running out of funds, or the golfer struggling to make it.

brilliant tip

Be hard-nosed. Will it be good for your business? Would something else be better?

In global terms sponsorship is growing because it links brands with pleasurable activity and reaches people in a good mood. If this works for you on a small scale think hard about it, but don't let the pleasure element confuse the rational decision-maker.

Sponsorship can be one of the early casualties in a budget cut (witness Honda and Formula One), so make sure the economic case for doing it is cast iron. Do not simply be taken in by an opportunity to associate yourself with your favourite sport or charity. Remember they want your money. Remember you want sales.

There are now so many new opportunities. Things you could never believe you could sponsor are now potentially available, from news programmes to all forms of entertainment. *Top Gear* is now a global brand in its own right. The world of marketing opportunity is wide open.

If you do decide to go for a sponsorship package for good cost reasons, one of which may be that this will increase your opportunities to develop your business relationship with some major customers, then that's a justification to go ahead. But whether it's a big or a small sponsorship, ensure that you maximise:

- Your branding.
- Your importance to the sponsor's marketing.
- Use of and exploitation rights of their key players – players and management.
- The guaranteed engagement of the sponsor with people in your company.
- Frequent (monthly) reviews of activity and its effect on your business.

Sponsorship is often a decision lightly taken and poorly seen through. Don't underestimate how much of your time it will take. But if you want to do it and can justify it on cost and impact grounds then really go for it – energy and enthusiasm will see you through. But one word of advice. Today's consumer is very smart so don't ever do anything tacky or inappropriate – you won't get away with it.

Key questions to ask yourself

Sponsorship is expensive. Think hard before getting involved in something that takes your time and gives back less than it should. Most sponsorship programmes that are disappointing are like that because no one admits or knows how much commitment successful sponsorship requires. Answer these questions honestly and you will make a better decision.

1 **What is the key marketing issue?** Is it brand awareness? Is it about making your brand, product or company seem more important than it is? Is it a consumer or a trade issue? Is it a global, national or local issue? Be clear about all of this first.

2 **Why are you thinking about sponsorship?**

3 **When you evaluate the option** in terms of ticking off the following, does it still make sense?

- Appeal to target market?
- Appeal to trade customers?
- Appeal to staff?
- Compares well with other options in terms of cost per person reached and in terms of influence and impact?

4 **How much is the most you can afford to invest?** Sponsorship can be very expensive. And remember you need to double at least the sponsorship cost to cover the marketing of it.

5 **Is this association going to improve the reputation of your brand?**

6 **Does the sponsorship fit with your strategy?**

7 **What ideas will make this sponsorship really different and exciting?**

8 **Are you clear about the personalities of the people you are sponsoring?** Could they be brilliant brand ambassadors?

CHAPTER 11

Designing a product into a brand star

n a world where all cars are designed in the same wind tunnel, it's the little things that make a world of design difference between two brands. As we learn in Walter Isaacson's biography of the late Steve Jobs, he was obsessed with design, with the curve of the iPod, with everything to do with how things looked and felt. This came from his passion for calligraphy and the sense of detail, shape and space that goes with that. Design has stepped up the marketing league table, not least because of Apple.

Designing a world of change

Designers were like engineers at one time, back-room boys who were craftsmen not to be trusted near executives. A series of geniuses including Michael Peters, Rodney Fitch and design companies such as Pentagram have changed everything. Now designers are, as a retail CEO put it, 'the first people I'd put in the lifeboat'. Companies such as JKR, The Partners, Coley Porter Bell and Sedley Place are at the centre – not the periphery – of building desire.

How design really works

Tom Peters said, 'Design is it!' By this he meant it was the key differentiating skill a company possessed in turning its functional products into sexy brands. It's what makes Tom love his

Stanley hammer. It's what Steve Jobs was talking about when he said 'the keys on the new Mac keyboard look so good you want to lick them'.

> **Design makes a big marketing difference … it makes things desirable.**

However good the marketing may be, if the product or service doesn't look great you will always struggle. That's why Absolut Vodka is such a marketing gift. What a bottle. Ditto the Boeing Dreamliner. Design makes a big marketing difference … it makes things desirable.

brilliant tip

Think about the little things and all the details that make a design 'look right'.

Imagine, if you can, the Microsoft iPad as opposed to the Apple iPad. Imagine Phil Green being let loose on Selfridges. Imagine most town planners being given free licence to develop Bath. Imagine what generations of brand managers would have done to Heinz Baked Beans packaging if designers hadn't stopped them. Design makes things desirable and keeps them consistent … it also makes executives in businesses actually think about how the way things look, feel, smell and sound will affect consumers. And especially it makes people realise it's a lot of apparently little things that combine to make up a symphony.

> **It's innovation that is at the heart of brilliance in design, marketing and business.**

Why 'I'll know it when I see it' isn't enough of a design brief

The brief is the tool that allows us to wrestle with the challenge, which in turn leads to innovation. It's innovation that is at the heart of brilliance in design, marketing and business.

brilliant tip

If you aren't trying to innovate you won't be brilliant in design, marketing or business.

The perfect product brief and packaging brief
Product

- What do I want my product to do that's different from what's on the market?

- How do I want the consumer to feel about this product?

- How modern or how traditional do I want it to seem?

- Do I want it to be multifunctional or focused on one key asset?

- How do I achieve a worried 'Oh no' from my competitors?

- How much simpler can we make it?

- Is there an irritating issue the consumer feels about products in this sector?

Packaging

- How visible does it need to be? Line up all competitive packs. (For a breakthrough example look at Yellow Tail outer packs for real stand-out design).

- How can I 'own' colour? The Heinz 'turquoise' is protected by trademark.

- How can I clarify the copy on the pack? By deciding:
  1 what must be on there
  2 what would be helpful to have on there
  3 what would be nice to have on there.

Packaging is about more than function. It is the 'face' a consumer or customer sees first (and as we know, first impressions count).

- Let's remember that packaging is about more than function. It is the 'face' a consumer or customer sees first (and as we know, first impressions count).

- Research shows as much as 75 per cent of purchases are made on impulse. (I actually doubt that statistic, but why run the risk?) So let's be brighter, more interesting and sharper on display. Whatever else, let's not be eclipsed by our competitors.

- For help contact the Design Council (www.designcouncil. org.uk), read *Design Week,* (www.designweek.co.uk) and talk to people who've had design teams working with them, so you can get a feel for who's hot or not. And if you need a low-cost local operation (very often they'll be excellent), look up 'Design Consultants', 'Design – Advertising and Graphic', 'Design – Product' under www.yell.com. There are 160 listed, for instance, in Brighton. Look to see what they've done and what you like. Create a shortlist and ask to see more of their work and listen to them talk. If you like what you hear and you like the work, talk to their clients to see what they think.

- Best of all, talk to people in business to get a few pointers. The desire to promote people good at anything is the best quality filter I know.

What has changed?

We've realised that how good we make things look, from the appearance to the pack design to the ambience in which we buy the product, actually makes a difference to sales. In the past, many people in marketing had slunk past the design issue but no longer. How things look, feel and smell are all critical because design differentiates.

John Deere is the most stolen tractor in the UK. Villains are queuing up to nick the green and yellow darlings. Ask them why and they'll tell you, 'It's the bleeding design, son, innit?' John Deere has the same charisma as Porsche and Bang and Olufsen. All of them exclusive but desirable and definitely not excluding. Henry Dreyfuss, the great American designer – he made everyday things look good, easy to use and unobtrusive, appears in the John Deere ads, where they have this great line about him:

'Say the name and every industrial designer in the world genuflects.'

Design is the amazing component in marketing.

Ask people why they buy Nike ... or Apple ... or Sony ... or Prada. Ask why that Amazon package that arrives in the post looks so great. Or the Dorset Cereal box. Or the Selfridges carrier bag.

Sit and look at them. Look really hard. I'll give you a few tips:

- Font
- Colours
- Authenticity of handwriting
- Product descriptors
- Simplicity
- And a sense of knowing who they are.

Design can make you fall in love

It does that to women with shoes and handbags all the time. It's design that does it (it sure isn't comfort). In the City of London young bankers have been seen with designer watches so heavy one of their arms is longer than the other.

Some people 'get' design, and some don't, but just for a moment reflect on the unutterable joy a 'just-right' design gives.

The Mazda MX-5 borrowed from the old sports-car character of the MG and other classic British sports cars and translated this into the late 20th century.

Virtually everything Dyson does, such as the Airblade hand dryer and the Bladeless Fan, looks great and works brilliantly.

Englishman Keith McNally has done it with the Balthazar Restaurant in New York, with its great atmosphere, food and, most of all, design.

Montblanc is the ultimate in pens. Very black, very shiny and they feel good in the hand.

We are talking beauty here, something elusive and out of reach. Albrecht Dürer said that 'there lives on earth no one beautiful person who could not be more beautiful'.

Brilliant design gets nearest to perfection.

brilliant tip

To survive in modern marketing you must stand apart and get people to notice you.

What great design does is fizz.

What great design does is fizz. It stands you apart from other stuff. It does half the marketing job just by being what it is. In their super book about design, *A Smile in the Mind*, Beryl McAlhone and David Stuart argue that graphics are made memorable by using witty thinking. What's more, they say, ideas that happen in the mind, stay in the mind. And I love this thought.

brilliant example

The story of the naughty chair

Managing director of design agency Sedley Place, Mick Nash, was asked by a teacher friend if he could solve a problem that was driving him and his colleagues crazy ... children leaning back on their chairs at school and spilling over backwards, often with injurious results. Mick said he could and did by designing a chair where the centre of gravity was located forwards, making backward-tipping a thing of the past. 'Ah,' said his friend, 'I should have mentioned the catch. They have to cost less than £20 a chair.'

'That,' said Mick, 'is not the problem. That is the brief.'

Good design is beautiful but it is also pragmatic and functionally focused. That's why it is so important in our lives.

brilliant tip

'What you need to know about a problem only becomes apparent as you are trying to solve it.'

(Richard McCormack of RJM Design)

Design is now centre stage

If you think about the most successful products, how they look is often key to their success, but increasingly what is happening is a rejection of over-design, especially when it comes to packaging.

From being a peripheral discipline, design has leapt to the centre of the marketing stage. A TV is not just a machine on which to look at programmes. It's an important focal

> Design has leapt to the centre of the marketing stage.

point in a living room. It's a piece of furniture. A car (unless you are Jeremy Clarkson) is not a virility symbol or high-performance machine but a statement about the new you. Look at the design of the Mercedes A6 or the Toyota Prius.

brilliant tip

'Give the client what he never dreamed he wanted.'

(Designer DewysLasdon)

Then take another look at Apple. Talk about love affairs because, like Stanley, this is what that brand's design inspires. And in the very dead of night you'll hear a John Deere starting up in deepest Essex, hopefully to the declamation, 'You're nicked, son.'

Design has leapt to the centre of the marketing stage.

And it's getting better.

What is absolutely clear is there's no excuse, with all the design talent around, for bad, ugly, cheap-looking design. The council tower blocks of the '70s were a disgrace. All the evidence is whoever you are and however much you earn, great design belongs to you too and can make you feel better and more valued.

Be like Marc Newsom, the brilliant Australian designer, who said we can always work to make design better.

Designing dos and don'ts

1 **If you are launching your own brand**, have virtually no money and are very brave then you can do it all yourself, but remember you'll have to live with it.

2 **There are just three things on which to focus:**
   i) Decide, define and brief what you want your brand to look and feel like.
   ii) Find other examples of what you want your design to resemble.
   iii) Don't be afraid to reject what you or your designers come up with ... it's easier to say 'no' now than it is later.

3 Here are some great examples:
   ● The Shell logo
   ● The Penguin paperback logo
   ● The 'I love New York' logo
   ● Harvey Nichols's Traditional Christmas Pudding, with the wrapping in the design of a large, old-fashioned sixpence
   ● The Jif Lemon packaging

4 **You learn how to be discerning** about great design by looking at great pack designs (Heinz, Kellogg's, Branston), or bottles (Gordon's Gin, Grey Goose, Singeton), or cover designs for books or products (Apple anything, Kath Kidston, White Company).

5 **Look at the way things are designed**, how they look and how they feel in the hand and eventually pennies will begin to drop and you'll start to see what works, what might work and even what's missing.

CHAPTER 12

Direct marketing – a world of data and innovation

Direct marketing has earned the reputation of being at the down-and-dirty end of marketing. It's a world of fliers, junk mail, personalised letters with lots of underlining, envelopes with photographs or tokens inside to stimulate the 'giving muscle' and a world of call centres in India bothering you on Sunday afternoon about some alleged problem you might have with your heating bill. That's the bad news.

The good news is we are trading direct more and more and the skills in this business are improving.

How direct marketing works

Direct marketing is about directly marketing to people on a one-to-one basis. It depends on creating and being able to process data so you can personalise your messaging to your audience in the most effective and economic way. At its simplest, direct marketing involves sending people coupons with offers (as Direct Line do), sending letters, doing telesales, and at its most sophisticated managing e-commerce programmes through web sites (as do Tesco or Amazon). Direct marketing first became highly favoured by clients in the 1980s because it is so clearly measurable – you spend 'x' and get sales of 'y', so your return on investment is easy to work out.

QED. Marketing is maths.

Your database is your radar system. By getting inside your
customers' minds you'll sell more efficiently.

What has changed?

The Godfather of direct marketing is Stan Rapp, founder of
Rapp and Collins (where he was CEO for 23 years) and now of
Engauge, an 'iDirect' agency. Stan was the writer of the seminal
book on direct marketing – *Maxi-Marketing* – published in the
later '80s. At the ADMA Conference in Sydney, Australia in
August 2010, aged 85, he was still giving it some about where
direct marketing is today.

*'It's interactive, integrated, informed, insightful, individualised and
innovative.'*

You're incredible, Stan, incredible.

This is what I love about the Americans – they never stop. So the
pioneering force in 1980s marketing (direct marketing) joins up
with the new kid on the block in 2008 (digital marketing) and
now, in 2011, 'iDirect Marketing' is at the core of the marketing
revolution. Or is it? Not quite, but Stan as ever is on the button
about using and not being used by technology. He says this:

*'Marketing is the total process for efficiently and effectively moving
goods and services from producer to consumer. Digital marketing
is as nonsensical as calling what happened in the 20th century
'analogue marketing'. Technology alone is not the best descriptive for
any marketing approach.'*

When he was young (a mere 61-year-old), Stan observed in
his book, *Maxi-Marketing*, the disintegration of homogeneous
consumer groups and the remorseless progress from mass

marketing to segmented marketing to niche marketing to one-to-one marketing. And the cheap tools to reach small groups or individuals. Today, accessing that information is virtually free.

He also said

'*The fascination with "creative" advertising is giving way to a concern for accountability and responsiveness.*'

I couldn't disagree more.

brilliant tip

A brilliant idea well communicated just once will always beat a deluge of junk mail.

The reason direct marketing hasn't been a bigger hit is its apparent 'determination to produce horrid and insensitive marketing pieces. Its fixation on the numbers has made it very left-brained and poor at reading the human psyche. Neither maths, nor drip-drip persistence, nor formulae will ever outdo a brilliant creative idea. And the good news in the 21st century is that the creatively discerning consumer and customer is king and that isn't going to change.

The customer is king

We are in a new phase of marketing that is virtually 'customised'. So when you order your new Audi or BMW it is customised to your order and then made. You can actually design your own Nike shoe online.

Direct marketing has a new opportunity. The ultimate consequence is interesting. It means if you have one million different customers you

Direct marketing has a new opportunity.

could (in theory) have one million different products, but you won't keep them in stock, you'll only make them to order.

Modern business can be what business in the 20th century could only dream about. This is beyond à la carte. We've gone from 'Any customer can have a car painted any colour that he wants so long as it is black' (Henry Ford about the Model T in 1909) to 'You name it, you've got it' (100 years later). And one of the key drivers to customisation has been direct marketing, because it allows one-to-one conversations.

Brilliant direct marketing means doing it better

Imagine a world where direct marketing was always witty, fresh and exciting. Imagine briefing your direct marketing people to produce material that was riveting, not just efficient. Remember, this is no longer megaphone country; this is quite an intimate one-to-one conversation. Imagine having a drink with a friend: telling jokes; telling stories; not talking too loudly; not showing off and selling stuff but giving the person you are talking to the chance to talk back to you.

brilliant tip

Treat the consumer as a person you like, would like to know better and want to talk with ('with', not 'to' or 'at').

Be persistent, of course, but sensitive in talking with your customers.

So is this soft sell? Softer – yes – and more in tune with what we know people want. Be persistent, of course, but sensitive in talking with your customers. The new way forward is in talking to about them new things. And not boringly telling them the same thing.

Brilliant direct marketing means being a data hound

I'm hugely impressed by direct marketer logistics and disappointed by the apparent lack of use of the data they must have. It's strange, but that seems to suggest they aren't terribly interested in their customers.

It was Duncan Watts of Yahoo Research who said in the second *McKinsey Quarterly* of 2011: 'Marketing is going to become a much more science-driven activity.'

That might be true at Yahoo but direct marketing stars such as Tesco don't engage me with intelligent conversation, although I'm a fairly regular shopper. Virgin can vary between brilliant and treating me like a stranger they pass in the street and fail to recognise. Others deal with complaints fantastically – too many to mention – so you'd be prepared to buy old socks from them but then they ignore you.

brilliant tip

Don't just acquire data; analyse what you have and act on it.

I think the trouble with science is it needs hard work, great process and intelligent users. So Duncan Watts is right in principle. In practice I suspect there are vaults of unexamined data files and missed opportunities and that direct marketing has not fully grown up to deal with this.

brilliant examples

1 **Buying books in the small hours.** It's midnight or beyond. Everyone's asleep. I'm sitting at my PC clearing up emails. I suddenly remember the name of a book recommended to me – *Alpha Dogs* by James   ▶

Harding – I must have it. On to Amazon. Ho, ho … £7 off. And … £100 and a pile of books later I press 'place order' and two days later the books I ordered arrive.

This is the best thing ever. They even gift-wrap the Christmas presents I send without my having to touch them myself. Amazon is a customer-service triumph and very impressive in every respect.

2 **Bose make the best hi-fi I know, with a great marketing presence**. They constantly mail me and do it properly. They have their top-of-the-range gear in the best shops. They have a trophy outlet in Regent's Street. Bose are the business.

3 **The best material and attitude of all is the Italian organic food company Fattoria La Vialli**. Their brochures are yummy and I feel guilty if I don't buy stuff. 'A presto' (see you soon), they write, and I feel part of their family. They are wonderful.

4 **Charles Tyrwhitt sell great shirts and excitingly bright ties**. They send out new catalogues all the time. It's a bit like having a well-dressed lodger in the house. Their tone of voice is relaxed and casual. Most of all I love Charles Tyrwhitt Wheeler's philosophy: 'I want to be the best shirt-maker in the world.'

5 **The new world of the middle class**. The women I know all shop online and widely:

- The scale of their shopping has widened in the last five years from about five suppliers to around 20.

- The top of the list are the White Company, Pure and Woolovers, but the efficiency and quality of service are generally good.

- The same trend has happened with charities – the number of charities given to has risen from three to 10. But many are marred by poor, old-fashioned copy and ghastly enclosures such as 12p stuck to a piece of sellotape or a pair of baby's socks.

- The persistence and insolence of call-centre staff are terrible. My own experiences have led me to role reverse:

  Q: 'Is Mr Hall there?'

Me: 'Hallo, this is Action Surveys – thanks for calling so promptly: how many seats are there in your contact centre?'

Q: 'What? Who? Er ... 350.'

Me: 'Good, thanks, and your location and the gender mix of your staff?'

This goes on until I ask:

Me: 'And do you like your job?' ... to be greeted with ...

Q: Sobbing ... 'No, I bloody hate it' ... (and out comes a life story).

That (as they say) will teach me.

---

brilliant tip

Be generous. Be kinder to your converts and to your existing consumers than to those you are trying to convert.

Why direct marketing can work

Direct marketing rightly finds favour because you can actually 'gauge' how it is working. This is marketing that accountants like.

> Direct marketing rightly finds favour because you can actually 'gauge' how it is working.

You can target consumers very specifically. Modern technology allows us to slice and dice data so we can build hugely complex but useful consumer profiles and models. This enables us, in theory, to spend our money much more effectively, only talking to the people we want to talk to and saying to each of them the sort of things they want to hear.

Direct marketing, as we can see in the alliance of direct and digital (iDirect), can be a key component in integrated marketing. But the real key is getting closer and closer to your customer.

Creativity sells. The trouble is the people who do direct marketing tend not to be focused on the quality of the creativity in their messaging, which is often dull because they are more into the maths of the subject than the fun of seduction. Put wit, freshness and vitality into the communication and something special could emerge.

Just because what you do can be measured doesn't mean you have to be dull. As Einstein said, 'Not everything that can be counted counts and not everything that counts can be counted.'

The key rules of direct marketing

1 **Your database is your power base.** It defines everything you need to know about your customer (their purchasing behaviour, their frequency of purchase, how much they spend and so on).

2 **Do the maths and you'll understand the general arithmetic of direct marketing**: 93 per cent of letters get no response and 40 per cent of all letters don't even get looked at, let alone read, and go straight in the bin. So you have to create a lot of activity to make a few sales: 1000 letters might get 70 responses, which might convert to 7 sales in the very end. The name of the game is to improve the maths by a mix of better material, better targeting, better offers, better follow-up, etc.

3 **This is a long game.** Marketing today is about building relationships. The term 'lifetime customer' is about someone who spends £20 a month with you and who could/should, therefore, spend nearly £10,000 over 40 years. The intimacy of the narrowcast direct-marketing relationship enables you to achieve what a broadcast medium can't.

4 **Become a flexible measuring machine.** Measure the

effect of every ad, of every activity, study the effect of everything you do. Discard what doesn't work. Retain what does.

5 **It's only called 'junk mail' because the content usually is junk.** As ever, be true to your brand. The materials produced by Johnny Boden, Charles Tyrwhitt, the Wine Society and the White Company are fabulous.

6 **Getting started means you need to talk to experts.** Always talk to experts, otherwise you'll end up creating a square wheel. Contact the Direct Marketing Association (http://www.dma.org.uk/) or the Institute of Direct Marketing (www.idm.com).

7 **Listening to experts is always smart.** Read *Sales Letters that Sell* by Drayton Bird, *New Maxi-Marketing* by Stan Rapp, *Secrets of Successful Direct Mail* by Richard Benson, *Profitable Direct Marketing* by Jim Kobs and, from the land down under where even violets don't shrink, *Direct Marketing Made Easy* by Malcolm Auld.

8 **Decide on your tone of voice.** This is you, not your agency, talking, whether in print or via a call centre to your customers and prospects. This is your brand, not their brand. Be you. Be in love with what you are marketing. Insist this tone of voice is consistent.

9 **We all do direct marketing all the time.** In the emails we send. In the letters we write. In the phone calls we make. It's time to reflect on how we can all make a more telling impression. For instance, have you thought of measuring how effective you are? What makes people stop, look and smile is where you can make a difference and stand out from the rest.

CHAPTER 13

Customer
relations
marketing –
it's people
who make a
difference

Business is full of good stuff about money, process and demand manipulation. McKinsey says there's been a multiplication of 'customer touch-points', which makes it all more complex, but customer engagement is the most important aspect of current marketing. And even big companies seem to realise people are changing, as Duncan Watts of Yahoo ruefully observes:

'Once you accept your intuition about how people behave is inherently flawed then you really need a different model for learning about the world.'

So focus on your understanding of people and your service skills or you'll suffer.

Customer service can make or break you

I'm not quite yet blue in the face (but very nearly) saying that it's getting the people-thing right that will get you marketing brilliance faster than anything else. You've got to hire the right people, coach these people, learn how to talk to people and respect people.

Getting the people-thing right will get you marketing brilliance faster than anything else.

Most of all you've got to love your customers.

brilliant tip

First impressions count. Walk into the reception of any company and the greeting and the energy levels tell you a lot about the company.

brilliant examples

First impressions

- When Saatchi & Saatchi first set up in business in the early 1970s in Golden Square in Soho their reception was about half the floor space of the whole agency. The back offices were small but the first impressions were of a big and successful business.

- Go into Abbott Mead Vickers, Marylebone Road, today and you get a feeling of freedom, youth and of a lot of business going on.

- Google HQ in Zurich is colourful, fun, witty and lively, with great sense of pride in the brand and of helping people perform at their best. And how about reclaimed and brightly painted cable cars as breakout rooms?

- And one not-so-brilliant first impression. A digital marketing company I saw recently had no one on reception so I wandered around until someone said, 'Who are you looking for?' I felt like saying, 'Don't bother, I'm a virtual guest.'

The British banks and service

Banks are not coached to like people or trust them. They're not places that like to say 'yes'. Until the credit boom came along, that is, and then they were falling over themselves to lend you money. But culture embeds deeply and the patina of the cultural woodwork is hard to change.

After the PPI scandal, in which it was discovered banks had sold customers £8 billion of unneeded insurance, people tried – at first to no avail – to get their money back. And then, as happens, one bank recanted and the floodgates of regret opened and repayment started. What it seemed to me should have happened is the service provider should have said:

'We thought we had this right.

But it turns out we didn't and we're very sorry.

We are delighted to repay you in full.

Please accept our apologies and we wish you well.

If there's anything we can do for you please call this number...'

Instead they grumpily and with bad grace wrote to customers protesting their innocence and outrage that they had to pay back the money. In the case of someone I know, the cheque he got was much bigger than he'd expected to receive but the way in which he received it left so unpleasant a taste he fired his bank once he'd cashed it.

brilliant tip

If you don't try and turn a complaint into a surprised and grateful customer you are missing a trick.

Customer service in small businesses

Imagine two restaurants both serving identical good food. In one the service is genial, fast and friendly, in the other surly, slow and stressed. Easy to choose where you'd go. Actually the food has to be quite a lot worse in restaurant one and your hunger really profound to even make restaurant two an option.

The restaurant analogy works for me. In running an advertising agency I regarded myself as the *maître d'*, my account people as waiters, the creative people as the kitchen and the creative director a heavily swearing, sweaty, red-eyed head chef distrustful of a world who sometimes didn't like his culinary expertise. The media people were like wine waiters who understood mysteries denied to most of us and decanted media plans, sniffing them as they did so. It's a fantasy, but the concept of CEO as *maître d'* speaks to me and to the need to place the customer at the heart of your business.

brilliant tip

Meeting, greeting, anticipating and looking after your customers' needs are skills we need to develop.

B2B service … where the buyer gets lost in the system

McDonald's skill at service is underestimated by some. The restaurants are easy to find, consistent in quality, you get what you ask for and the price is set. Compare this with a design or advertising agency. You meet the boss once. The initial work is terrific. Then you meet junior people who don't understand what they are selling to you and there are lots of hidden extras. And you feel a bit unwelcome … especially if you complain and then you are probably made to feel ungrateful or stupid or both. The brutal truth is quite a lot of creative businesses are only semi-house-trained, as it were.

The art is to run a happy shop that is open, confident and on the customer's side.

The way you treat your staff will affect the way they treat their customers. Sam Walton, founder of Walmart, said it took less than a week for nasty management to corrode the behaviour of front-line people. The art is to run a happy shop (most good advertising agency heads still call their agencies shops) that is open, confident and on the customer's side.

People as brands

We need to personalise the whole branding thing. The killer question, which can be asked of yourself or your company, is this:

'Who are you (now)?' Not who were you or who would you like to be but who are you NOW?

JesperKunde, the Danish marketer and author of *Corporate Religion: Building a Strong Company*, says this:

'Branding is about the company fulfilling its potential, not about a new logo. What is my mission in life? What do I want to convey to people? And how do I make sure that what I have to offer the world is actually unique?'

brilliant tip

You can't always choose what you do. But you can choose how you do it.

Interestingly, people are unique, although in large companies we often seem determined to train them into clones.

Look at the big people-brands of the past ten years: Steve Jobs, Jamie Oliver, Carla Sarkozy, Madonna, Helen Mirren, Shane Warne and so on. All of these stand or stood for something. Linda Barker thinks she is a brand and describes herself in the third person, which is a bit weird, as I remarked to Richard Hall just the other day.

In politics the personality of the candidate plays a major part. Does the camera love them? Do they have smiling eyes? Do they look honest? Politics plays out on TV mainly and Boris Johnson has the touch. You feel he says (come what may) what he thinks.

How to improve your relationship with customers

1 Hire the right people. When you hire people, think of yourself as a 'casting director'. Your corporate brand needs a mix of talent, not just one sort of person. But if they don't fit in, don't hire them, however great their CV. At Google they interview everyone 20 times – just to make sure they are getting it right.

2 Help your people play to their strengths, which is what brands do. Ben & Jerry's doesn't waste its time talking about its slimming credentials. It lives in the land of Yum. Make sure everyone is clear about what you stand for in simple English.

> Hire a great receptionist. They are the signpost to a company.

3 Hire a great receptionist. It's a really important job. They are the signpost to a company.

4 Learn how to smile. You could try practising. Smiling is an art: it's not an occasional habit.

5 Create an office that stands for your brand decoratively and in terms of layout. Encourage people to make where they work dramatise their brand values.

6 Remember people's names. This is something everyone in a business needs to do effortlessly. If you remember your customers' names they'll remember you.

7 Meet all your customers once or twice a year and get them

to tell you how you score along a whole variety of axes, including the following:

- Efficiency
- Effectiveness
- Improvement (or reverse) overall
- Are they made to feel appreciated?

You can do this as an email check. (Try to avoid six-point scales as I recommended three years back. This is about getting a broad picture of satisfaction or the reverse; it's not, as in ice skating, about getting a score.) But you need to follow it up with a one-to-one conversation as well, so that you can say 'thank you', make immediate changes that are needed and so you can read between the lines, which is often where the most interesting information is hidden.

8 Money spent ensuring you constantly train your people (and yourself) to be better at customer relationships will not be money wasted. Like presentation skills, it's all too often taken for granted.

Customer service – making it a human thing, not a process

You cannot hope to be brilliant at marketing if you don't deliver brilliant customer service. Even if you are a waiter, work in a call centre or as a sales representative. You get out of life what you put in. Being great at customer service is one of the best and most fun jobs there is. The best people should fight their way to the front, trying to outperform their peers at exceeding customer expectation.

brilliant tip

Try to see things from your customers' viewpoint.

How brands can distinguish themselves is by the quantity and quality of goodwill they bring to their customers. And remember bad service is always anecdotal and devastating. For example: the fish dish in a well-known restaurant in Brighton was much too salty for my wife's taste. We told the *maître d'* who took it away and then brought it back saying 'The chef and I have tasted it and it's fine.'

brilliant tip

If you genuinely don't LOVE your customers, how on earth do you expect them to LOVE you and your brand?

Keeping them, not just winning them

The art of keeping your customers is underestimated and it isn't easy in a competitive world; but keeping them costs a fraction of the cost of winning new customers. And whilst keeping them doesn't seem as sexy as winning new ones, it's your number-one need in building a sustainable business.

I've used this statement so many times but, as you'll be discovering, one of the weapons of brilliant marketing is repetition. Charles Orvis said:

'Your customer's right even when he's goddamned wrong.'

The top ten of customer relations

1 **People are changing**, which is making customer engagement harder and more important.

2 **Hiring, coaching and working** with the right kind of people are key.

3 **First impressions matter.**

4 **If you make a mistake, say sorry** nicely, fix it and try and repair the trust.

5 **Front-of-house** should always be front-of-mind.

6 **Suspicious customers** are like that because you've allowed trust to go.

7 **Smile.**

8 **See things from the customers' point of view.**

9 **Love your customers**; they are feeding you.

10 **Keeping customers** is more important than winning new ones (although you always need new challenges).

CHAPTER 14

Marketing the noisy, sensual and surreptitious way

We have a whole bunch of underutilised tools at our disposal. We have the technology to really give shoppers an exciting brand experience. We can appeal to all the senses and cause a real stir. And we have our wits so we can ambush people with music, performance or events in the street or on buses that bring a brand laughingly in front of them. Marketing can be smelly, bright, noisy or fluffy – it's up to you.

> Marketing can be smelly, bright, noisy or fluffy – it's up to you.

Experiential marketing: senses to bring your brand to life

Experiential should do what it says … play with the senses. It's been on the verge of happening for years but I realise in the three years since I wrote the first edition of *Brilliant Marketing* nothing much seems to have happened.

Maybe the trouble is it's a 'nice to have' rather than a must-have. Maybe my vision of a heather-floored dome with the cry of grouse, the sound of a waterfall and the scent of chilled, Scottish air with a running film of Scottish Highlands scenery, clouds scudding across the ice-blue sky, as a tasting venue for a new malt whisky brand just won't happen. Or maybe it will … why not?

brilliant tip

When the others zig, you must zag.

How experiential marketing should work

This used to be called merchandising a brand. Now it's potentially a serious science. It allows you to dramatise your brand sensually and far more excitingly. This is theatre, where the customer experience is raised to a high level of interest. As such your opportunity is to be theatrical and amaze and engage. This is 21st-century merchandising. Brilliant experiential marketing is potentially very sexy.

What is changing?

1 **There's a need for something different.** What most marketers are currently doing would have been OK in the past but now we live in much more discriminating times. Theme parks, films and video games have heightened the point at which our senses respond.

2 **Retail can be more than a warehouse experience.** Technology has moved on so fast we really can create virtual-reality situations. Very few of the obstacles that once stopped us doing convincing experiential marketing exist any more. Shoppers need to be wooed a bit more cleverly.

3 **Premium brands need love.** In the spoil-yourself world of expensive mega brands, the experience of seeing how they are romanced is phenomenal in the great New York stores. This is branding at its highest level.

4 **Our brains are changing.** Susan Greenfield believes that years of internet exposure have changed the way we think. I agree. We need to stretch ourselves with fear

(theme park rides), taste (new world foods), new sensations (fish pedicure), new 3D films, adventure holidays, great surround sounds (water, storms and birdsong) and more.

A short sensual adventure

Let me take you on a short journey, a journey through some of the most wonderful department stores and shops in the world. Share with me the 'rush' of excitement a great shopper experience and experiential marketing can deliver.

- La Fromagerie, Moxon Street, Marylebone. It smells wonderful. The shop has a long, shared table in their tasting café. Sacks of succulent, speciality potatoes lie rumpled on the floor. It's a world of quiche and sun-dried aubergine. First and last this is a cheese shop. The 'cheese room' is a cornucopia of smelly delight, with the hiss of the humidifier in constant action.

- Selfridges. Actually the whole store owes more to the world of magicians and caves of treasure than it does to retailing. Its ethos is indulgence, and they are indulging millions of pounds to make their point. It's pure theatre. Its credo is indulgence. And expertise. Talk to the girls in Clarins and you are talking to skin experts.

- Experiential for pets. A German pet food company, Affinity Petcare, had posters that said 'Listen to your nose' at pet height. Behind the posters they placed fresh pet food, the smell of which was emitted through small holes. Lots of dogs sniffing. Lots of interested owners.

- ScentAir: spraying a scent of baby powder in baby departments of stores shows sales go up as a result. ScentAir have now gone into partnership with Muzak – sound and smell in harmony.

- Castlemaine XXXX has created Truckmania and the Gold Retreat, a big two-storey bar that is assembled quickly from the back of a truck to provide a bar, terrace and stage on which brand lovelies create a dance floor so everyone can party – and they do party, drinking lots of beer in the meantime.

● Prada in New York: experience effortless superiority and rich minimalism. Its vast sweep of wooden boards descending into an undulation of mannequin displays and then rising again has to be seen to be understood. And do you feel different about Prada after going in there? I actually wanted to buy stuff in there – anything ... that's how good it was.

● Dean and Deluca in New York – a temple dedicated to delicatessen delight.

Adding a new dimension to presentation

Experiential marketing is about leveraging the sensual aspects of a brand. When you do it well and memorably it's brilliant. The need to stand out in a retail environment makes one wish for more weapons. Technology has come on so far you can do almost anything. We all want experience at first hand, which is the reason the best theme parks have done so well and why investment is going into revving up the buzz. But it's not just theme parks. The demand for live performance is soaring. The O2 Arena is a roaring success.

> The demand for live performance is soaring.

Today live experience is the thing. Customers expect it and relish the experience.

> Customers expect it and relish the experience.

Buzz marketing – when everyone starts talking about you

How 'buzz marketing' works (or marketing as we used to call it)

The idea of getting talked about predates marketing. You get talked about by breaking the mould and being attention-getting. What it stands for today is something that turns enough heads in enough places and that gets a brand on the mental map. It will usually take the form of a weird idea in action, a happening (an unplanned event), a stunt or an idea that grabs people's attention and gets free media. This is definitely not textbook stuff. There was once a newspaper headline, 'Freddie Starr Ate My Hamster' – it wasn't true – that was buzz.

brilliant tip

Remember who's in charge – the consumer. Kevin Roberts (again):

'For the first time the consumer is boss, which is fascinatingly frightening, scary and terrifying because everything we used to do, everything we used to know, will no longer work.'

The implications of customer power

We shall have to work with the consumer more closely. This is going to be more like marriage than marketing. Now we have to look for more interactivity and sharing of brand ownership with them. As the Coca-Cola fiasco with 'New Coke' in 1985 showed – consumers and customers are in charge. Coca-Cola also discovered the brand is stronger in consumer hands than bottler hands.

What is changing?

When I first entered marketing, this category was described as 'below the line'. For the purposes of simplicity I'm going to enclose 'buzz', 'ambient', 'guerilla', 'high impact' and 'stunt' marketing under this broad category, which signs up as a cousin of PR and event marketing.

Its current fame is a result of its being embraced online because it's so easy to broadcast a come-to-this-now on Facebook or Twitter. It is cheap creativity. However, what it represents and stands for is the kind of bravery of attitude that Nike or Snapple demonstrated early on in their existence.

How to be noisy

> Brilliant buzz marketing is all about getting attention.

Brilliant buzz marketing is all about getting attention, then surfing the wave of public interest and getting a smile:

- Publicise a vegetarian restaurant by putting a sandwich board on a calf that walks around and proclaims 'Make my day. Eat at Cranks.'

- A bank manager in a midwest town of America dressed in white with a mask to launch his new system of home loans and who rode his white horse down the high street at a gallop: 'The Loan Arranger Comes to Town.'

- The 'Will it blend?' series on YouTube for Blendtec is a blast and a buzz. Watch them actually blend an iPad. GEICO Car Insurance and Blendtec both push the boundaries of silliness and make £1 look like a lot more.

brilliant tip

Being worth a mention means passing the 'You won't believe this but ...' test.

- Carlsberg mounted a 'We don't do litter' campaign, which comprised dropping £20 notes randomly on to London streets each bearing a sticker on which that campaign message appeared (budget £5000).

Word of mouth is not an accident – you have to work at it, just as you have to work at fame. Creating buzz is achieved quite often by doing the really counter-intuitive thing.

NOT BY BEING NOISY LIKE THIS.

But like this.

(Whispering loudly.)

Unlocking the buzz

- Be relevant – if you aren't on the consumers' radar screen you can't cut into their consciousness. You'll just be noise.

- Be accessible – if you aren't their kind of person then however good the message you have you'll struggle. Example: M&S trying to reach most teenage kids = disconnect. Facebook trying to reach a 70-year-old = tricky.

- Be different – being ordinary is 'soooo boring' ... zzzzzzzzzzzzzzzzzz. 'Same as ... same as' is not news. So unless you do your buzz idea with originality you will sink expensively and to deserved snorts of derision.

How to focus on key people to maximise the buzz

Focus on 'opinion formers', people who can enlarge and embellish your story. Identify the people in a group who can dramatise the message, those whom Malcolm Gladwell, best-selling author of *The Tipping Point* and *The Outliers*, calls 'mavens'. Understand what will make them 'look and laugh' and create a buzz by enrolling them, the talkers and gossip spreaders, as your 'buzz force'.

Run chat rooms where your customers can criticise you. Remember that the truth is your strongest weapon. And spread the word. Always use 'tell a friend' instructions – buzz is a constantly interesting conversation.

Be exciting and don't be a control freak

Buzz marketing is like skating on black ice. A bit dangerous but awesome when you pull it off.

You will never get word of mouth going by being ordinary. Some, like Innocent, aren't ordinary. You have to take a few risks, because once the buzz is going you have lost control and the consumer will take over anyway. Buzz marketing is like skating on black ice. A bit dangerous but awesome when you pull it off.

Some of the most interesting 'buzz work' has been done by 'flash mobs' – strangers coordinated by text to appear at a given public place and act out some performance then leave.

IE (Improv Everywhere) appear in New York and have now acquired some fame for repeating a five-minute sequence of events in a Starbucks coffee shop over and over again for an hour. Or by flooding a Best Buy store with members dressed exactly like the staff. The thought of walking into a store and having five store-uniformed people surrounding you saying,

'Can I help?' – 'No, can I help?' – 'Please let me help' and so on, is wonderful and memorable.

brilliant tip

Actors are cheap and are brilliant. Get a bunch to work on a buzz with you and see.

A choir in Holland publicised a concert by assembling surreptitiously as ordinary members of the public, one by one and in little groups, in a shopping centre and spontaneously bursting into brilliant song.

How strategic can you be?

Here's where the Nike School of marketing, the philosophy of which is 'If it isn't damaging and if you like it and you think the consumer will like it too, just do it,' runs head on into the marketing attitude of a Kodak or Heinz, who will do nothing if there's a strategic disconnect. In the end you have to value how positive the buzz will be in relation to the time and effort involved because, ultimately, the return on your investment really does matter.

brilliant examples

Spontaneous events and happenings: these are what Ben & Jerry's did, brilliantly, creating parties on the web or by text, inviting people to sample their products at a given place at a given time. Someone who worked with them said one of the keys was they were very generous in sampling.

There's a story of 'ambush marketing' in which Nike usurped the main sponsor, Adidas, at the Atlanta Olympics by simply buying up all the trackside posters and poster sites in the city for the period of the Olympics. ▷

Unsurprisingly this was a one-off. At the Beijing Olympics, for instance, all the poster sites were held by the governing body, who then sold them on to sponsors. At the London Olympics write Ben & Jerry's on your forehead and you could end up in gaol!

Agent Provocateur = sexy lingerie – quite a bit naughtier than anything else in the high street and that wonderful line 'More S&M than M&S' did the business for them. Great PR and, like Avis with Hertz, always clever to compare a small brand with a huge brand.

Sony Ericsson's new, improved mobile phone with a great camera was promoted by actors who got tourists to take photos of them with this brand new object and then explained the product when the tourists asked questions. (This is sort of 'reverse-chugging'.) Word got out that something new and interesting was about. People started talking.

The Drive-U-home Service – the guys doing a 'We'll drive you home in your own car if you get pissed in this pub' service advertised above pub urinals for just when you are reflecting that driving might be a really bad idea, should hopefully have done well.

brilliant tip

Pay to change a bit of landscape and create a story. Like green postboxes or yellow London taxis. Or paint a town pink like they did for Barbie. A real talking point. Or plant a wall like GE have done in Trafalgar Square. They're saying GE is a green company now.

In Belgium there's an event in a cinema when young couples arrive late for a movie to be seated in the last two seats amongst an audience of 148 aggressively tattooed bikers. When they eventually and successfully clamber over these belligerent men to their seats they are spot-lit, the cinema erupts in applause and now-beaming bikers hand them each a Carlsberg. And up on the screen – 'That calls for a Carlsberg.' A funny and heart-warming idea.

Brand pigeons – a genius painted brand names on the breasts of pigeons in Times Square. Not popular with animal lovers. But it got talked about.

Cool target marketing – The stunt pulled by DDB (the advertising agency) for VW in 2004 was to sculpt a full-size car in ice and place it parked in a London street. It took 12 hours to melt.

Brilliant word of mouth: gather round and listen

● **Where:** The places where buzz occurs will be in the street, on public transport or in a public space, not in conventional media.

● **How:** The idea of buzz is to ambush the consumer with an idea they find funny (in his own way, the best example of buzz in advertising was that funny orange Tango man who went around smacking people).

● **Who:** The key in 'buzz' is to target tightly, especially opinion formers who'll pass it on.

> The key in 'buzz' is to target tightly.

● **Who's in charge:** Remember you can't guarantee being in control of it. You are setting something up that may be taken over by the consumer. Look at Facebook parties.

● **What:** This is the world of jokes. A good joke gets everywhere in hours now. Does your buzz idea have those legs? Buzz is for younger rather than older markets.

● **Checklist:** Is the core idea broadly brand-relevant, easily accessible to the consumer and different?

Most of all, 'buzz' is fun and pantomime. Serious brands which take themselves very seriously hate it.

Buzz is for the rebellious and those who want to make £1 look like £10.

Top ten experential and buzz marketing

1 **Appeal to the real hidden persuaders** – people's senses. No one's doing this well right now.

2 **Live performance and the experience of new** is a key driver in our lives.

3 **Why let luxury brands hog** the experiential limelight?

4 **Make sampling your brand an adventure**, not a 'touch-point in the marketing journey'.

5 **Get people talking about it** by giving them some fun.

6 **Think up ways of putting your brand on stage** or putting it up in lights.

7 **Talk to opinion formers and mavens.** Excite them. Get them talking.

8 **Don't be cheap** because the medium's cheap – invest in style but in a maverick way.

9 **The best event always ends as a brilliant party.**

10 **Think young, think wacky** – get some excitement going. Buzz has no zzzzzzzzzzz in it.

CHAPTER 15

Selling – turning marketing into action

Odd, isn't it, that so few marketing books have chapters on selling in them, when without sales revenue we are all dead and buried, however brilliant our marketing plans? In *Guerilla Marketing*, Jay Conrad Levinson talks about salespeople as a breed of commission-only mercenaries: 'if they ask for a salary, be nice to them and say no'. The word 'salesman' is not always meant as a compliment. When someone is described as a 'bit of a salesman' it implies they are a sharp-talking huckster who'll stop at nothing to get a deal. And in the sub-prime mortgage selling of complex 'financial instruments' to whomever the City salesmen could offload the things, we saw the worst side of selling. The City and telesales between them have damaged the reputation of selling more than anything else.

brilliant tip

Your customers' trust in you is your most precious asset.

But most salespeople are straight people whose careers depend on them being trusted by their customers. They are, and seek to be seen as, professionals. This chapter aims to put right the poor image some spoilers have given the profession once and for all, and to re-establish the salesperson as a key and leading member of the marketing team.

Finding the right people

Malcolm Gladwell, in his book *The Tipping Point,* describes salespeople as people capable of spreading ideas. He says:

'It's energy. It's enthusiasm. It's charm. It's likeability. It's all those things and something more'

The something more, he'd say, is 'irresistibility'. But Malcolm is American and he is seduced by the American vision of selling, which he more fully describes in *What the Dog Saw* – a collection of his New Yorker articles in which he describes the art form of QVC Shopping Channel 'pitching' as immortalised by genius salespeople such as Ron Popeil. Gladwell tells the story of how, in just his first hour on live TV (demonstrating, presenting, cooking and taking phone-ins), pitching the new, promotional version of the Showtime Rotisserie, Ron sold a record $1 million of product:

'It was one thing to talk about how Ron was the best there ever was …but quite another thing to see proof of it before your very eyes … (enter Ron Popeil from the TV studio after that first hour) … there was a hush and then the whole room stood up and cheered.'

The hair at the back of my neck stands up when I read this. It would for anyone who's sold or pitched.

brilliant tip

One day you'll get that sense of being an unstoppably compelling salesperson - train for that day.

There's a heady moment when you can visualise nothing stopping you and no one capable of presenting you with an objection you can't sweep aside or, better, twist to your laughing advantage. You feel immortal and at one with yourself. You are unscripted but feel as though you are presenting a divine script and you enjoy being in your own company. You want people to buy from you because it feels like the right, the only, thing to do.

Selling is the last bastion of optimism and opportunism.

Salespeople are not whingers (and if they are they won't last long). Selling is the last bastion of optimism and opportunism.

Selling B2B

A salesperson of high-ticket merchandise to commercial customers will be different from someone working in retail, as will a salesperson working with a big brand company where reputation and trust have been built over time. Someone selling medical equipment or high-tech products is a sales consultant whose primary objective is to create a relationship, not achieve a one-off sales transaction.

No one effective in sales today aspires to be anything less than:

- A brilliant presenter.
- A brilliant relationship-builder.
- A fount of deep knowledge in the product sector.
- An assiduous listener.
- A business strategist.

brilliant tip

To be a brilliant salesperson, be an expert, a businessman and a brilliant presenter.

Increasingly top salespeople are global salespeople too. The premium this puts on being a profoundly knowledgeable and compelling presenter of a product portfolio is obvious. In government circles the belief that 'being better at selling is the single most important thing we can do for the economy' has taken deep root.

The art of sales planning

The other side of selling is more rational but, in a topsy-turvy world, critical. And that's the ability

All great salespeople are great at planning.

to juggle, predict and do a tightrope walk all at the same time. All great salespeople are great at planning and understanding their customers' businesses and they have an intuition about timing. The time when it's right to push, when it's right to make a concession and when it's right to stop.

Great sales planning is about breaking down a sales forecast into manageable, meaningful chunks. A target of £1 million breaks down to £4,500 a working day (or just £550 an hour). It represents £10,000 a customer if you have 100 of them. It spreads a lot of ways.

Targets are never fair nor are they precisely scientific. They represent the opportunity for a good salesperson to work out 'how to', not to wonder 'if'.

> **brilliant tip**
>
> Working out how to use time, your local knowledge and your customer base to achieve a sales target requires a skill and positivism you'll need to develop.

The art of sales planning lies right at the heart of brilliant marketing because, however good a marketing plan, it won't happen if the people selling to customers aren't motivated and equipped to do the job. The relationship between a salesperson and a marketer is like that between an actor and a producer. The latter gets everything in place but the actor has to be given a good script, proper direction and the room to interpret what will work for the audience.

The art of sales planning lies right at the heart of brilliant marketing.

Plans should not be short-term things, however the economy booms and busts. Brilliant salespeople are playing a two-handed game. On the left-hand side filling the sales pipeline, getting orders, confirming orders and following up. That's the transactional stuff. And on the right-hand side developing and building relationships, acquiring competitive and marketplace intelligence and creating a sales framework for the future. That's the intelligent stuff.

brilliant tip

Selling is marketing in action. Marketing people need to spend more time with salespeople.

Professional salespeople always have a plan and know how to use their time and the opportunities so their performance is never erratic. We spend too little time praising salespeople. And marketing people spend too little time on a one-to-one basis understanding and working out with salespeople how to tap into the real opportunities in the marketplace and build partnerships with key customers. It's time that changed.

brilliant tip

Listen to your salespeople. Ask what their customers want, why, what for, how much and do not patronise or confuse them. Give them what their customers want and need.

▶ brilliant | example

Why I hate high-tech shops

The real lesson here is that the guys in shops do not speak my language and make me feel everything's my fault, not theirs. They are not salespeople; they are the equivalent of traffic wardens, there to stop you doing anything the store dislikes. They are there to upsell, cross-sell and confuse. And they don't want my money ... they do not want me to 'buy happy'(as Norwich Union put it). When we went to buy a computer for my wife we came home empty-handed, frustrated and bemused. I called my IT man who came round, he sat with my wife, chatted through what she needed and we shopped online through Laptops Direct. It took 20 minutes. We spent £500. The kit arrived the next day. It wasn't hard.

Selling in the 21st century

Here are some examples of how selling is changing:

1 Tesla is the leader in electric cars in the USA. They are starting to take off. The Tesla Roadster actually accelerates faster than most sports cars, yet produces no emissions. Apple and Gap executive George Blankenship is joining them as vice president of design and store development. Having managed the growth of over 250 Apple stores worldwide his job here is to build Tesla's retail strategy and network. Tesla stores are also the service hub for Tesla Rangers, the mobile service programme that provides house-calls for service. Tesla Rangers travel to customer homes or offices to carry out services, including annual inspections and upgrades. So eat your heart out, Jeremy Clarkson, having been so rude about the Nissan Leaf on Top Gear.

2 The word 'conversation' is new (we seldom hear the word 'pitch' nowadays.) We all avoid formal, bullet-point

presentations. Instead, we have conversations. Increasingly, 'selling' is going to be about customising things so they fit the buyer rather than suit the seller ('Any colour you want so long as it's black' is history).

3 Selling 'now'. Today you specify your car and wait several weeks until it's made. It doesn't need to be like this. Nor do banks have to take five days to clear a cheque. The real selling story is going to revolve around quality, value, relationship and *speed*. If you or your business isn't overnight-fast you are probably not going to be reading this.

brilliant tip

The world is getting faster. It's time to work out how you can speed up what you do. Speed gives you sales edge.

4 Taking customers to experience mind-changing places to precondition the selling process. Here are just five I've heard about recently, all involving going behind the scenes:

● At a premier division football club stadium.

● At the Globe Theatre.

● At the Whitehall War Rooms.

● At the ICMA Trading Centre at Reading University.

● At the Royal Opera House.

5 We'll have fewer but smarter salespeople who spend a lot of their time working out how to improve customer performance with their brands. They will be doing what marketing people used to do in the past and acting as consultants.

6 The new pitchers of the 21st century are quieter than they used to be. American Adam Lisagor, a success story as

a commercials director in the USA, has espoused a style that is quiet, spare and deadpan. He believes his audience – the new consumer – is smart enough to want to hear a cool story being told without hype. Which suggests the salesperson of today is going to have to learn a variety of styles of selling.

Thinking small

In running a small business the owner or the boss will be the primary salesperson. They will have the benefit of being especially passionate and knowledgeable about their product or service. All they have to learn is how to be distinctive and effective as a presenter.

The essential skills are no different, but in a small business we are looking less for a polished professional and more for the sort of person Margaret Heffernan, author of *Women on Top* and the champion of women entrepreneurs, describes as having an 'irrational love of their customers'. In a small business someone who spends money with you is literally keeping you alive. In small businesses the simple art of selling yourself and your product is at the heart of marketing, not a service to it. That's what Ron Popeil did on QTV. That's what great leaders of business can still do. It's what made Steve Jobs so compelling a leader. He was a great salesman and he positioned Apple as an accessible business bringing you magical products. Ron and Steve had a lot more in common than anyone might think.

brilliant tip

Love your customers and love the fun of telling them the story about your product and company service.

Often the best salespeople wouldn't recognise it if you told them they were great salespeople. But they all have the following things in common:

- The appetite to listen and to empathise.

- The passion to tell a good story.

- The belief in what they are selling – I was once told you could only tell a great salesperson by how well they sold rubbish – which is rubbish itself.

The reputation of selling has taken two knocks – from telesales and from financial salesmen offloading exotic 'instruments'. But at its core, and ignoring these mavericks, selling is a noble profession and becoming more important.

Technology is transforming everything, most of all our access to information and the ability it confers on our getting faster and faster in

> Real human beings rule and sell OK.

responding to customers. Delivery times are getting shorter. But one thing is not changing: the need for face-to-face contact. Real human beings rule and sell OK.

The rules of selling

1 Being trusted by your customers is vital.

2 Being an irresistible storyteller is a huge asset.

3 Enjoy 'pitching' – it's fun and having fun is infectious.

4 If you aren't an optimist find something else to do.

5 You have to be smart and knowledgeable to be a salesperson – no one will know your product from a customer perspective better than you.

6 The art of sales planning lies right at the heart of brilliant marketing.

7 Make it easy for people to buy from you ... why is it so many make it harder than it should be?

8 Cultivate your marketing and financial colleagues – the better you all get on, the better the company will do.

9 Selling is becoming more to do with business strategy and is more conversational than hard sell.

10 Think long-term relationships with your customers, not short-term sales.

CHAPTER 16

Creating an integrated marketing plan

There's so much choice it's very confusing. What's needed are the ability, experience and skill to put together a balanced plan that is a 'recipe for success'. It will need to give you the coverage, the frequency of impact, the flexibility and the opportunity for creative excitement that you want. This is where we are looking for an integrated plan.

Mapping the explosion of choice

It's constantly said choice, in our lives today, is the creator of stress. So pity the marketer who's hearing the voices of advertising, PR, sponsorship and branded entertainment, buzz and experiential marketing, CRM, design, direct marketing, digital and social marketing – all of them beguilingly begging to be included in the plan.

How to plan

If you are small, do the plan yourself and take an arbitrary number of activities – two or three will do – and link specific activities to one central idea.

If you are a medium-sized business, do the same.

It you are a big business, maybe add just one other activity.

Keep the 'What we need to do' and 'What we could do it with' lists short in all instances. Less is always more.

How to buy

If you can, use
professionals to help.

If you can, use professionals to help. Buying anything is done better by them.

If you have to do it yourself:

- Explain you are small.
- Ask for the professionals' help.
- Get them to say what they think they can sell you their space for and then ...
- Get a second opinion over a drink with a professional buyer.

But if you don't have a great central sales idea, capable of grabbing attention, all this is an academic exercise, like writing a book well but with a bad plot.

Getting the central idea right

Putting all your eggs in one basket always seems risky, so if you do, watch that basket! Get professionals to produce your marketing programmes (advertising, design, PR and sponsorship etc.) since it's rare for an amateur to produce anything that has the power a professional will achieve. However, sometimes you have no choice. Here are a series of things to help if you are doing this yourself.

Read your own brief

Your brief is your exam question. Take a big A2 pad and start to generate ideas. Relax, scribble short phrases – anything that catches the eye and is on the brief. After an hour or so, hopefully you'll have a few thoughts that are worth pursuing. Whatever you do keep the options simple and have everything lined up to a big central idea. You'll have to do this more than once to get good stuff flowing.

brilliant tip

If you can, work with someone else sometime during this process to check what you are doing.

How people get their ideas

Like all artists they beg, borrow or steal them. As Picasso said, 'Amateurs borrow, professionals steal,' but if you watch them, senior creative people in advertising agencies read more than most people, listen to more music, visit more art galleries and watch a lot more films than average. They are rather like 'creative blotting paper'.

If you have an idea you like – it could be a headline or a picture – show it to your wife, husband, child, mother, father, friend, whoever and get a reaction. If in doubt, reject it. And reconcile yourself to a harsh reality of life: this is hard and may take quite a long time. But if you think you've cracked it, leave whatever you've done and come back to review it 24 hours later.

brilliant tip

In the cold light of day what seemed genius at 11.30pm sometimes reveals itself in its true colours as being garbage at 11.30am only the next day.

What hooks people?

It's about connecting with them; creating an echo in their brain; doing what nursery rhymes do to young children. It's about assonance or alliteration or rhymes or reference to something else or a piece of wit. Here's one of the oldest advertising lyrics ever:

'You'll wonder where the yellow went

when you brush your teeth with Pepsodent.'

This may not be poetry but it's a great commercial verse.

Making marketing agencies do great work for you

You don't get to work at a marketing or ad agency unless you have what someone I know calls the 'smarts'. Jeremy Bullmore, who is one of the cleverest men to have been in advertising, describes creative people as wearing black T-shirts and looking permanently grumpy. In my experience they are often quite insecure, wondering if they can still produce great work and feeling only as good as their last advertisement. One of them told me his greatest terror was that the next ad just wouldn't come.

brilliant tip

Help those insecure creative people feel loved and rated. Ask that they have lunch on you, the client.

Agency relationships

Make sure that the agency values your business, not just because you spend money with them but because you are appreciative of their skill and effort. Thank them. Make them pleased that you are coming in to see them. Go out of your way to be popular and then be as demanding as you want, which should be very demanding.

Make sure that they understand what you are trying to achieve in the long run, not just on an ad-by-ad basis. Agency people are professionals and like dealing with people who have grand plans, who have a strategic vision. And they like feeling they are working in partnership.

And make sure that they know you like good work and want to sponsor stuff that is cutting edge and will make them look good with their peers.

> Use experts but have very strong opinions yourself.

brilliant tip

Use experts. (The worst media planners are amateurs and untrained media buyers are dangerous.) But that doesn't stop you walking around with your eyes open, seeing how different people consume advertising in different places in different ways. Use experts but have very strong opinions yourself.

Where to advertise so it reaches the people you want to reach

Know your audience

Describe them in detail. The choice of media today is such that you can be much more rifleshot than grapeshot in your aim. List your different types of audience: what they think, feel, do, aspire to, enjoy as hobbies. Really try to get inside their minds. We are way past defining people with boring old demographic titles (C2 female 35–45). Now we want to know what she really thinks and where she lives.

How much do you have to spend?

How sensitive is this? Is that the maximum, minimum, antici-pated, agreed or whatever budget? Don't do loads of work until this is clear.

Answer the following questions:

● What are your preferences for types of marketing and why?

(A professional will dissuade you if he genuinely thinks you are wrong.)

- What is your long-term strategy and what is this particular campaign trying to achieve?
- How important is stand-out for you?
- Have you considered being very noisy and active with a smaller group rather than trying to reach a wider audience?
- Have you thought about being counter-intuitive and trying to find a really unusual and creative way of achieving your goal? (Good integrated marketing is not just about maths, it's also about imagination.)
- Are you being sceptical about measurements such as CPT (cost per thousand)? Think more about cost per customer conversion – i.e. if you spend £x how many new users do you need and how much extra usage from existing users? (Arithmetic in terms of ROI is critical.)
- How do you see the schedule of activity contributing to the momentum of the campaign?
- Which components are designed to achieve what?
- Consider this is a building – what are the foundations? What is the roof?

Investigate mainstream media

A quick gallop through the media scene with some opinion as to what is going on may provoke some ideas:

TV – the biggest sales tool ever invented.

Cinema – magnificent, if you have the wit and creativity to compete with Hollywood films.

Radio – said by many housewives in research to be their best friend. An underused medium.

Posters – patchy distribution makes it hard to reach many in places such as Cambridge or Brighton, but for me, done well they are one of the classiest ways of making a statement. Advice: if you are focusing on a specific town make sure you know where the best sites are. The best sites are where people are waiting – at a station, in a predictable traffic jam, at traffic lights.

National newspapers – this is where your ads become tomorrow's fish-and-chips paper. The best ads I've ever seen in newspapers were always newsy and topical. Circulation is declining fast.

Magazines – a totally different browsing world with a vast choice of specialist titles.

The web – it has its own chapter, of course. Just make sure your web site works properly, and through intelligent SEM make sure you are in the right place on the page – near the top.

Local newspapers – the underestimated medium. The creative environment is often quite dull so standing out can be quite easy.

Free sheets – I am a deep sceptic but check out the prices and make your own judgement.

Local magazines – focus on the feel and the quality of editorial; do not just rely on the numbers.

Transport – for little money in London, tube cards and cross-track can be absolute magic. It's one of the few chances to have people read your quite long copy because they haven't anything else to do.

Events – easy to get swept up and find you are having a great time, but sales of your product remain disappointingly flat.

Theatre/event programmes – generally don't.

YouTube – brilliant for mailing links to 'warm contacts'.

Sponsorship – if it isn't spot-on right, avoid.

DM – only if you are sure you have a great idea that works on a one-to-one basis – better for B2B brands.

Design – are your packaging, product design holding you back?

PR – what can they do with stories in your business? Your mission is to dig out a lot of juicy new stories.

Buzz – a headline stealer? Are you up for the risk?

Experiential – sexy marketing. Can you pull it off? Is it right for your brand?

CRM – could a coaching programme transform your salespeople?

Buying your media is risky

Same advice. If possible, find a professional to do it for you. But if you can't then you are in the 'hot seat'.

Unless you are a great negotiator get someone else to do it for you. In life, avoid trying to be a 'one-man band'; the music they produce is usually terrible. But if there's no choice, get out your calculator, put on your ruthless shoes and start buying. Here are five pieces of advice:

1 Be tough but nice.

2 Be knowledgeable. Only try and buy something when you have lots of information – the ratecards of your chosen media and all the competitive media.

3 Be smart.

4 Be professional.

5 Keep it simple. Don't ever try to orchestrate a programme of events that keeps you lying awake at night.

brilliant tip

Spend a useful lunch with a media professional who will give you right up-to-the-mark opinions and facts about what is really going on in media.

Creating the right plan

> Be excited by what you are doing – this is great fun.

Be excited by what you are doing – this is great fun – and it's more fun because it isn't easy, so the satisfaction of doing it well is enormous. Remember the advertising idea and expression of the 'short-sell', that two-word equity – the piece of territory we are going to make unique for our brand – that distilled message for your product, service or brand that is the platform that underpins everything else.

Get that right and you're nearly there on the road to brilliance.

But also remember this is about money and measurement and getting enough bangs for your buck. This is about thinking with your whole brain – left-brain scepticism plus right-brain creativity.

And building a structured campaign that makes sense.

Integrated marketing checklist

Here are the key questions. Do you have:

1 **The right people** working with you?

2 **The right weight** (of money)?

3 **The right message?**

4 **The right mix of media** to reach as much of your target market as you can?

5 **Clear objectives** (what do you want your target market to do)?

6 **The right time** to pitch your brand at the market?

PART 3

How to create and execute a great marketing plan

However clever and creative you are, money is preciously guarded by banks and financial directors and you'll find it hard to get hold of it unless people think you know what you are doing, where you are going and what the return is going to be.

So you need to know how to put together a persuasive, well thought-out plan. That's a given. But so is a bit of excitement.

CHAPTER 17

Achieving
momentum
– the art of
marketing

This is thrilling stuff – marketing. I can't imagine why all bright creative people don't want to play. Just don't let the grim-faced money-men put you off being you and enjoying it too. The consumer is not a statistic, she's your mum, he's your dad – we're talking friends here, we're talking a diversity of people, but we're talking about people, not just about numbers.

How to create momentum

The single most difficult thing to do in life is to make things happen. Achieving momentum involves enrolling popular support, doing things that get noticed and persuading people to think about you and your company differently.

Momentum involves something changing. When M&S changed the look of their stores and the prototype store got pages in the papers,

> Momentum involves something changing.

reviewing it rather like a film is reviewed, they acquired momentum.

The same with the launch of the new Kindle ... something new was happening.

And, on a smaller basis, the queues outside Le Relais de Venice in London, where they don't take bookings and only serve steak (great steak) asking, when they come to take your order, 'How would you like it?' not 'What would you like?' – the queues say it all.

Rihanna took her top off to film a promotional video in a field in Ireland, enraging a farmer and hitting the headlines. That was real PR momentum.

brilliant tip

If your people are slowing down, find a reason to celebrate – throw a party and create momentum.

The concept of 'party' was brilliantly explored by Rory Sutherland, vice chairman of the Ogilvy Group UK, when he speculated the £6 billion spend on high-speed Eurostar rail-track might have been better invested in supermodel waiters and waitresses serving Chateau Petrus – 'people would have wanted it to go slower if we'd done that and we'd have had about £3 billion left over'. There are more creative things to do than get there 40 minutes sooner.

Get the right team

Good marketing people have one thing in common – they enjoy people, the stories they tell, and they love advertising. The best advice in finding the right team to work with is to ask these questions:

- Will they fit in and make you better?
- Can you get on with them?
- Do they share your energy levels?
- Are they positive-minded? (I personally can't work with cynics.)
- Are they restlessly ambitious?

Oren Jacob, who used to run IT at Pixar, says the sort of people you should be looking for have these characteristics:

'Three traits: humor, the ability to tell a story, and an example of excellence. These aren't unique qualities to assess in applicants, but how excellence is defined is not that common. It doesn't matter what you are excellent at, just that you have reached a level of excellence. It's important that you know what excellence feels like and what it takes to achieve it. It could be gardening, jujitsu, or cooking. The main thing is you've had a taste of excellence and will know how to get there again.'

Learn from the best

Listen to the best, read stuff that inspires you and if it doesn't inspire you stop reading it. Who are the best to listen to or read right now?

Seth Godin – author of *Purple Cow* and maybe the best thinker around

Rory Sutherland – Ogilvy's answer to Stephen Fry

Professor Sean Meehan of IMD – marketing guru

Dan Cobley – marketing director of Google

Adam Morgan – author of *Eating the Big Fish*

Sophie Patrikios – Lego CRM director

'Why don't we talk more about B2B?'

Sorry, we should have, or should have stopped you getting the perception that I was ignoring B2B, but I don't think there's such a big distinction between B2B and B2C. People are people, after all.

I've spent my life in journeys working between breakfast cereal, hi-fi, beer, car parts, trucks, cars, insurance (personal lines and corporate), hotels, professional services, government services and foods such as sauces and ready-to-eat meals, and as they say in 'Will it blend?' – check this on Google – the answer is 'Yes – all good marketing thinking blends into one question':

How do we make our customer – whoever they are – do what we want them to do?

That's the essence of marketing.

The only difference is good B2B marketing is often more to do with business consultancy and tailored problem-solving than marketing techniques. It's where the best salespeople morph into marketers, and the concept of the lifetime customer becomes the Holy Grail.

How to keep on running

1 **Speed at work and in marketing** matters because ours is not, despite Roy Sutherland's winning words, a leisurely society. We are all demanding next-day or even same-day delivery. We want it great and we want it now.

2 **Part of everything we do now is related to perception** – adding apparent value. That is the magic that marketing can weave. We can take a sow's ear and 'Hey presto' here's a silk purse ... actually it's still a sow's ear but a branded one and we now see it in a silky light. Thus it is with speed. There is no role for the slow.

Tell great stories and be incredibly fast in what you do.

3 **So apply the art of marketing**. Party. Celebrate. Enjoy. Tell great stories and be incredibly fast in what you do.

CHAPTER 18

Key steps in creating a plan – the science of marketing

There's no virtue in pretending you can do more than is feasible. Examine the limitations of your budget, resources, production capacity and the appeal of your offering. Then, when you decide, forecast or guess (most of business has elements of inspired guessing involved) what your sales are going to be and what you need to do to achieve them, make sure the plan you aim to achieve looks 'realistic'.

This doesn't mean to say you shouldn't be ambitious and try hard to beat your forecasts. Just don't overcook it. You'll regret it if you do.

brilliant tip

Don't try and fight above your weight, which could prove futile and painful.

So decide who you are and the limits of your ambitions:

> So decide who you are and the limits of your ambitions.

1 Are you doing DIY marketing with a small budget and is what you are involved in a 'one-off' with hardly any pennies to count?

2 Are you in a small business (maybe even your own business) where every penny really counts?

3 Are you in a middle-sized company trying to be a bigger company, with a sense of being squeezed by retailers or distributors and where every penny is important?

4 Are you in the marketing department of a big marketing company with access to professional resources (both internal and external)? You should still have an 'Every penny has to count' attitude, but there are a lot more pennies and your options are somewhat more extensive.

In life we all discover everything is relative, so don't try and be a big company marketer in a small parish church and don't design your own posters in a big company.

Headline questions

Before you write the brief for your plan, think really hard about the following questions. Because in a busy, busy world we spend too much time rushing around and not enough time thinking. Here are some simple, get-that-brain-working questions:

1 What are you really selling (or look at it the other way – what are people buying from you)?

2 What are you really trying to achieve?

3 How hard is this going to be?

4 Why?

5 Are you sure your key objective is right?

6 How much money and other resources do you have to achieve that?

7 Over what period of time are you trying to achieve it?

8 What's your simple central story or message?

Remember you are just laying foundations. This process is

one where a sudden blinding insight can transform everything. But this is the professional way of starting the process. Thinking, kicking things around and asking the probing questions.

> This process is one where a sudden blinding insight can transform everything.

Writing the brief

Briefs are not called brief for nothing, so keep it short and to the point. The discipline of writing a brief will focus your mind. It would be great to get it down to just two or three pages. The aim is to have a simple piece of writing that is so clearly written a stranger will understand precisely what it is you want, need and are looking for.

brilliant tip

Sit down with as many people as possible who stimulate or inspire you to talk about your brief.

The selling message is the key to success

Great, simple sales pitches can inspire your imagination, your feelings or your brain. Just don't be too subtle and don't be boring.

Think of the great sales messages of our time. Castrol isn't just oil, it's 'liquid engineering', which implies this is the real McCoy – the one the pros understand. Carlsberg used to say it was 'probably the best lager in the world' – the word 'probably' is heavy with irony: probably = definitely agree or I'll thump you (probably). And, in a cynical world, how about Innocent saying 'We sure aren't perfect but we're trying to do the right thing'? That's better than Google's 'We do no evil' because, try as they might, they do – sometimes. Mind you, they do more good and are big, busy and innovative enough to get away with it. But if I were them I'd nick the more honest Innocent approach.

Refining the core selling message is critical.

Refining the core selling message is critical. If you have 'true intent', expression of it will always be concise: 'We are going to win;' 'We are one of the most exciting companies in the world;' 'We are the best shirt-maker in the world;' and so on.

Focus on the 'what it is', 'why you need it' part of the message. Do not allow yourself to be accused of producing a message that has people saying, 'I didn't know what your product was for and what it did.' And always think about where the message will be seen. Is it likely to be where you have a captive audience or where you have to shout to be heard or do something really creative?

brilliant tip

A new way of looking at brilliance is that less is more.

But whatever else you do, keep it short.

I loved Picasso's comment to a man who saw him next to a large lump of marble and, on hearing that Picasso intended to hew a horse head from it, said that looked like a jolly hard thing to do. Picasso replied:

'Not really, what I have to do is chip away the bits that don't look like horse – that's all.'

Brilliance in marketing is about chipping away, finding and being thrilled by new possibilities. So let's get chipping.

Present the plan as though you mean it

Presenting your plan to a board, investors, a business partner, or your wife or husband whom you want to buy into your decision to stop looking for a job and start a new business instead, needs to be treated seriously. And it needs to be done with confidence, style and thoroughness.

> **brilliant tip**
>
> Check your plan for any holes. Ask yourself 'Would I buy this?'

Presenting a plan shouldn't be a process – you should give those to whom you're presenting 'an experience'. Be creative. Do it somewhere unusual. From the top of a high building – talk about perspective, vision, being above the battle – or have a meeting in the Cabinet War Rooms and talk about the competitive strategies you are facing in your 'brand war'. Or do it in a box at a local football ground where, looking at the green striped grass below, you can talk about the big words in football – commitment, possession, pace and creativity.

Now present it really fast

Like me I expect you hate jargon, which I've tried my best to avoid. So I hate the phrase 'elevator pitch'. The last time I was in a lift and someone said 'Can I pitch you an idea?' my heart sank and I lost concentration, because that's just old-fashioned interruption selling.

Write a script – think 'Twitter-short' – and divide it into three parts:

1 **Why** people want what you have.

2 **How** your product is better.

3 **What** makes your marketing likely to succeed.

Be creative. You're allowed to start 'My grandmother hated Marmite but she loved Vegemite so I thought…'. Get thinking – personalise the consumer – be interesting.

Never stop planning or expecting the unexpected

Plans are not written in stone. As the increasingly impressive JM Keynes said to someone criticising him for changing track:

'When circumstances change, I change my mind, sir. What do you do?'

brilliant tip

Be prepared to tear up your plan.

A plan is just a plan. Things can change. Be prepared to review on a very regular basis to be sure nothing needs tweaking or changing. If it does, change it. It's that simple.

Why small plans are the best ones

The Google headquarters I visited, companies such as Apple (which feels like a company I know rather than use), call centres such as BUPA (who sound like they know you), all act small. Acting small means they are all into detail – your name, your history – you, not a number.

Great businesses remember … that's one of the key differences between good and bad businesses. Good ones remember. Great ones remember and know all about you.

In writing your plan put in an extra section, 'How we must plan to make our customers feel special'. This may be the most important part of the brief. It's also the biggest opportunity that small businesses have.

brilliant tip

Remember all you can about your customers (especially if you're small). The other guys have what they laughingly call a database; you have memory and humanity.

1 **Your product or service.** What is it, what does it do, who is it for, where do I get it, why is it good, who is the owner/promoter of it and what, in a nutshell, is it all about?

2 **What is/are the unique assets, characteristics of your product?** Also list and explain all the characteristics that may not be unique but are still interesting and worth talking about. Try and identify your 'key message'. This is your opportunity to be passionate, excited and exciting. Sell yourself.

3 **What does your consumer think?** Is there any research? What are the good and not so good things? See if you can define what it is that is most important to the potential consumer. How do you think your consumer or customer feels, as opposed to thinks, about your product? How do they use the product? How do they buy it? Who are they? Why do those who use it like it?

4 **What can we learn from sales?** Where, when and why do they peak or trough? How do you achieve them? What does anyone at the sharp end of sales say about what's needed?

5 **Your competition.** Who and what are they, how do they compare in price, quality, presentation, people, star appeal, benefits and size? What do people think about them? Which of you'd win in a stand-up fight and why?

6 **What does this campaign have to do?** Does it have to sell something, open the door for someone to sell

something, merely inform, change a given group's opinion about something or so on. Avoid the temptation of asking for more than one thing to be done. And if you can't do that, isolate the most important task.

7 **What specific challenges need to be overcome?** These might be the economy, recent competitive activity, adverse news coverage, your competitors' weight of marketing spend, or suspicions that your product is inferior to other products, anything – this is our 'Please be honest' time.

8 **What will success look like?** Put a number on it: sales; market share; penetration increase; distribution gain; PR stories. Don't be vague. Be brave.

9 **What's your budget?** Ditto.

10 **What other resources do you have?** People (employees or volunteers), free material, premises, anything you can think of ...

CHAPTER 19

The ten brilliant ways of managing people and your campaigns

1 Be a champion
Every marketing initiative needs a champion, someone
who'll go way beyond any call of duty to make it succeed.
No great champion = no great campaign.

2 Team is all
Your team (internal and external), united by you, is what
will make this adventure succeed.

3 The weekly inquisition
You need to meet or talk weekly (and briefly)to make sure
everything is working properly and in a coordinated way.
This is truth time. Don't bury bad news. Tell it and fix it.

4 Diversity works
Your team needs to be diverse, not just clones of you
(however good you are). When you really try to get the best
out of a diverse group of people something extraordinary
can happen.

5 The 'fact monitor' keeps you in line
You need one person (or if there is only you then you need
to find half a day a week to do it yourself) to make sure all
the factual stuff (actions, dates, emails) all the left-brain
stuff, is done and recorded.

6 First-hand is truth
This is not about failing to trust people. It's about getting

out and checking stuff first-hand. It's about smelling the
coffee. Not trusting all will be OK.

7 If you don't fail you aren't trying hard enough
I don't do 'failure'. I do 'learning from surprising
outcomes'. I do pushing to limits. I do finding out where
comfort zones stop.

8 Don't be frightened of changing things
If it isn't working, change it. Never be frightened of
changing stuff – it's a sign of great strength. And don't
always be impulsive. Sometimes waiting is a good strategy.
Trust your gut.

9 Get feedback
Ask people what they think. Never stop showing people
what you are doing. Listen to their comments and think
about them. They may be wrong but they'll usually be
useful.

10 Celebrate with gratitude
The most powerful words in management are 'thank
you' and 'well done'. Find reasons to celebrate success.
Stopping, having a beer and laughing will make you better.

PART 4

The real world, strategy and creativity

This real world is better than fiction. It's chaotic and that won't change. Speed of reaction is increasing in the video game of our lives. We need to be reactive, visionary and creative. We need to visualise what might happen next and learn from our mistakes. Most of all we need to be pragmatic. In uncertain times even plans written in titanium can get changed. Especially when it comes to money.

CHAPTER 20

That dreaded budget cut

M oney is always tight. But the so-called tensions between the finance and marketing functions are the normal tensions that exist when searching questions are asked about return on investment (ROI). And it's more complicated now because so many CFOs are getting better at understanding the way marketing works.

Ultimately, business is about generating more money than we spend and ensuring what we do spend is well and prudently spent. Owing to this pressure that we spend well and almost certainly need to find savings during the year, any smart marketer is going to be well versed in how to save money and, perhaps even more importantly, how to defend critical areas of the plan.

> Any smart marketer is going to be well versed in how to save money.

Here are some pieces of advice for when you are creating, defending or being besieged over your budget:

- **Be transparent**. Make sure whoever is funding your marketing investment is given the courtesy of proper explanation so that before the event they know exactly what they are in for. This will save much angst and confusion later on.

- **Be calm**. This is business, as Don Corleone in *The Godfather* quipped. It calls for clarity and focus. Do not be overly protective. Be dispassionate. There is a lot of talk about 'passion' in business. Passion does not belong in a conversation about money, especially when someone is trying to take it away.

- **Avoid waste**. Marketing is a bit like a fuel-thirsty car revving up with a Ferrari-like exhaust at the traffic lights. It consumes forests of documents, vast electricity bills of PowerPoint presentations and, of course, travel and entertainment are a well-thumbed expense category. Be careful about all expenditure. Become a new puritan.

- **Get it right the first time**. The downside of the endless quest for perfection is that money flows away on projects that are refined and re-refined. Don't spend a penny until you've asked lots of questions about where you are going, why and when.

- **Do a theoretical exercise privately**. On the basis that a budget cut is almost inevitable, envisage how you'd respond. Cutting the budget may be the necessity demanded by the CEO. You're a marketer – how do you fix the sort of problem you're liable to be served up with?

- **Become more ROI-obsessed than the finance people**. The name of the game is 'What-do-I-spend-and-what-do-I-get?' Be completely fixated on answering this question about all your people and resources: 'Am I getting the most

I could out of them?' Can you make £1 work like £10? This is all about relationships and unselfishly understanding the needs of all your suppliers.

● **How do you handle variable workload?** Freelance. This is when getting in real, temporary talent really pays for itself. Make sure you have a list of brilliant people who can help out, and if you can't think of anyone go to the local Chamber of Commerce and ask them, or alternately put a request for help out on Facebook or LinkedIn. Some of the people who might be able to help are young mothers who have great experience and who can work from home.

● **Spread versus depth**. If your budget, in common with all others, is going to be cut by a blunder elsewhere in the business or through economic circumstances, be grown up. Consider maintaining the quantity of impact against a smaller universe. Better by far to prove your plan works in a concentrated version than that cutting investment by top-slicing means it simply fails through lack of fuel. Critically define to whom you want to talk much more precisely than you have done so far and you can save money. All modern business is about choices.

● **The real world is tough**. Building a budget, guarding it and saving sums within it are all part of the skills of being a brilliant marketer. Do not, however, get upset when they want money back halfway through the year ... help them, and think hard about how to solve their problem as well as yours. Just being an easy victim isn't a smart ploy. As George Osborne (irritatingly) said, 'We're all in this together'. Make sure it isn't just you in it.

Managing money matters

1 **The task of a great marketer is to deliver results** and to create a plan that does that. But money is the root of all

Money is the root of all
marketing plans.

marketing plans, so you have to be great at the money, not just at the creativity.

2 **Be transparent, be calm but most of all be creative.** Show how marketing can help internally as well as externally.

3 **Don't delude yourself by cutting so deep** (as asked) that you simply kill your plan by denying it any oxygen. Saying 'no' is never popular but it's better than 'Yes I'll cut but I'm an idiot.'

4 **'We have no money so we shall have to think.'** We can always try saying that, and it's strange how well it works (just don't tell your finance director).

CHAPTER 21

The creative accelerator

'Creativity is the last legal way to gain an unfair advantage.'

Maurice Saatchi said this, and in so doing put creativity on its proper pedestal. Creativity, clever thinking or thinking laterally, horizontally – anything but in straight lines. Human beings have learned to be ingenious. It's up to us to exploit this.

What is creativity?

Creativity is magic. It achieves the unexpected. It takes us to new places.

> Creativity is magic. It achieves the unexpected. It takes us to new places.

Yet very few understand what creativity is or how to value it and fewer know how to be creative. There is some bizarre impression that random *non sequiturs* may be creative and that you have to be crazy to be creative.

But this is changing. Creativity is now on the management agenda. In fact, the art of creativity lies in making connections, in cross-referencing ideas so people start to think in a different way. Creativity is about being relaxed enough to have lots of ideas, not just one great one.

At the very heart of brilliant marketing is a series of ingredients, but most of all, and most excitingly, is the creative idea

– something that is in some way inspirational and that catapults the objective you've set yourself into engaging in real action. Is it likely to create momentum, a sense of something changing? Creativity lies in words like 'Yes, we can' – thank you, Barack.

brilliant tip

Practise laughing - tell jokes, look at funny commercials. Laughter and creative thinking go together.

Laughter and creative thinking go together.

There are certain preconditions of being creative:

● a right-sided brain on red alert

● a fully attuned sense of curiosity

● a lot of material to play with – a blank sheet of paper alone is not a good thing

● a sense of the need to produce something

● laughter

● being yourself

● taking a deep breath and asking yourself 'yes' or 'no' – often the answer simply comes to you. (This last one comes from Professor Michael Ray, Stanford University – try it.)

brilliant tip

Always listen to your inner voice (you may have 50 reasons to do something but if your gut isn't saying 'yes', don't do it).

Why creativity matters so much in marketing is because we're trying to do quite difficult things – to be noticed, to change opinion or to strengthen opinion, to provoke action. We are not going to achieve those (especially being noticed) by being recessive or ordinary. Human beings like creative things. They like clever things. And they like funny things; hence the runaway success of that TV series *QI*.

▶ brilliant examples

- Skype – making talk free and easy.
- The Oyster Card – making travel simple.
- Use-by dates on food – the biggest contributor to increased food sales and better health.
- PayPal – making paying for stuff online safer.
- Prius – put solar panels in their car roofs because they discovered a lot of their owners were prone to have a snooze in their car at lunchtime and wanted the air conditioning on but didn't want to leave the engine running.
- Prêt-à-Portea at the Berkeley Hotel – wanted to do something creative for ladies who'd lunched and now wanted to have a stylish tea. So the people at the Berkeley created designer fashion biscuits, with each designer contributing to the colour and shape of their own range.
- Boutique camping – the progeny of years of Glastonbury. Really comfy tents that are brilliantly appointed. Luxury loos and shower blocks are now provided at key events. Sleeping in the open air is the new 5* experience.
- Two from M&S – Airflex soles that are incredibly comfy and diminish foot odour in shoes – (air conditioning for feet) and 'coin-catcher' trouser pockets designed to stop your change falling out.

The power of creativity

As a nation, creativity is what we are really good at – best at advertising, best at marketing (and about to get better) and highly inventive (Dyson is one of many, and the chief designer at Apple, Sir Jonathan Ive, is British). So our opportunities as designers, inventors and simply at being cleverly creative are enormous. We need creative-ideas-villages, not business parks, and we need a lot of them, so that one group's ideas can rub off on another's.

> The magic of creativity in marketing is to find a new way of packaging an old idea.

The magic of creativity in marketing is to find a new way of packaging an old idea. It's about getting people to notice, say 'wow' and pick up the product. Creativity allows you to think about, see and feel things in a completely new way. It's what creativity does, not what it is, that matters.

Learning how to be creative

So how do you get into the creative zone? Here's a ten-point programme that can begin to turn you from a corporate duckling into a suave, creative swan:

1 **Creative identity**
   Think about two ways of introducing yourself to a room of people – the safe way and the dramatic way. 'My name is Richard Hall. I have worked in marketing, advertising, leadership and coaching …' zzzzzzzzzzzzzz

   Or 'What on earth was I thinking about, giving up a nice solid job as a client to join the debauchery of advertising?' … That's slightly more promising.

2 **Choosing creativity**
   Visit a shop and seek out two things you think are really creative and decide exactly why you think that is … find two things, by the same token, you think are really boring.

3 **Think about creativity**
   Now do the same thing with two different kinds of art. But

they must be different – music and poetry, a painting and
a play. Ask yourself just why they stand out. Also question
why you like them and see how many interesting or relevant
things you can say about them.

4 **Journey into creativity**
   Now go on a journey walking down a high street near where
   you live with a camera, taking pictures of anything that
   strikes you as interesting. Try and create a story around the
   ten most interesting pictures and how they enable you to
   describe the way the world is changing and what's going to
   happen next.

5 **Creative abundance**
   Don't be suckered into believing during the initial creative
   process that less is more. Less is less. You need to fill pages,
   walls, rooms and mansions with your stuff. Prolific is good.
   Take a product, any product, but especially, for preference,
   one you like and write down in an hour on a big A2 pad
   as many different marketing ideas as you can think of that
   might increase sales. Then spend an hour picking the half-
   dozen or so that seem to have the most promise, and then
   spend another hour polishing those.

6 **Creative teams**
   Fact is 1 + 1 = 3. Yes – synergy applies. That's why you
   have creative teams in advertising agencies who are both
   copywriters and art directors – their roles often cross over.
   Try working with a kindred spirit whose opinion and
   creativity you respect.

7 **Fast-forward creativity**
   Occasionally in a crisis you need to be able to come up with
   a bunch of creative options in very little time. Let's suppose
   you hear a competitor is about to launch a well-priced
   product that competes with your main profit earner. This
   needs an exciting and fast response.

8 **Mobilising crisis-creativity**

When you have a specific challenge get a group of front-line operators together from call centres, PR, your advertising agency, your receptionists, salespeople, finance people. For a few hours get them to debate the challenge and report back their solutions. You'll be amazed how brilliant they are.

9 **Take lots of baths**

It wasn't just Archimedes who found baths useful. In a world of showers our creativity is under severe threat – so get in that bath and let your mind roam. The key is to wash away the spreadsheet cobwebs that corrode marketing today; and if you want to be really inspired just look at YouTube and the best commercials.

10 **Meeting your consumers**

And just maybe the most creative thing you can do is to get a bunch of your consumers together and have a conversation with them – maybe even over a beer or a glass of wine. You'll learn a lot.

CHAPTER 22

Market research in this real world

What is market research?

t is the technique of looking at and understanding customers' attitudes and their behaviour in all aspects of considering a brand. Research is about measuring and diagnosing. Research is your radar system. It is there to help you, not to make decisions for you. But a good research insight can lead you to a brilliant place.

> Research is about measuring and diagnosing.

But there's a problem. Research is used politically so people in business can blame the consumer ... 'Well, they said...' to substitute for the marketers' own failure to think.

'Most people use research much as a drunkard uses a lamppost – more for support than illumination.'

(David Ogilvy)

And I love this from the late, great Anita:

'Using research to manage a business is like using the rear-view mirror to drive a car.'

(Dame Anita Roddick)

We know that research is, at best, a pretty blunt tool. We know that asking, 'What do you think of lavatory paper?' is unlikely to provoke a useful or even a truthful answer.

brilliant tip

Apple doesn't do research.

We have seen a diminishing credibility in the accuracy of political polls, with the remarkable exception of YouGov – due in part to its being completed privately and online. Doing things online tends to make you dispassionately honest in a way a normal questionnaire doesn't. An expert recently described the web as a 'disinhibiting environment'.

brilliant example

This original piece of research was conducted online in August and September 2011. The objective was to see what 18 senior marketers felt about their jobs and the context in which they were operating.

These were the 10 key findings:

1 Most who thought marketing important thought digital was now the number-one medium.

2 Twenty-six per cent thought marketing was unchanging or reducing in importance, but all those who thought marketing was changing thought it was changing a lot.

3 The integration of the whole armoury of tools was seen as key. There was felt to be a critical need for a coherent, clear marketing strategy.

4 Time was the biggest issue. Twenty-four-hour news. Pace of change. Stuff that would have taken 15 days to produce a decade ago is now expected in five days.

5 There are a lot of technically competent people around but few great, all-round marketers.

6 There is a decreasing amount of money to spend on marketing right now.

7 The marketplace has changed from one of artful persuasion and a seller's market to a buyer's market where marketers are now more focused on listening than talking.

8 There's an increasing movement to face-to-face marketing, especially in B2B.

9 Ideas still matter and people who have a bit of magic up their sleeves are at a premium.

10 Twenty businesses and their marketing campaigns were mentioned as leaving an outstanding impression. Only four had more than one mention, and I guess I was surprised (pleased, actually) by the diversity of choice, proving that great marketers are individualists. Here are the top four:

i) Apple

ii) Sainsbury's

ii) Waitrose

ii) Geico

Old-fashioned research is history

Would we have had the fire or wheel if they had undergone market research?

There was a series of films created by the Idea Group in San Diego about focus groups held with cavemen. (Check it out on Google.) The first was about fire, which to a Neanderthal they agreed would be better if it were cool not dangerously hot, and more symmetrical, and if it were green not red, which is too aggressive a colour, reminiscent of blood and death. If there were a cool green fire I might buy it, one said. So fire, as we know it, got the thumbs-down; as did the wheel, which they thought might run away downhill and hurt someone. So much better, they agreed, if it were square – much safer. Watch it – if nothing else puts you off focus groups this will. It's a brilliant little campaign, very funny and pointed, but most of all containing terrifying notes of truth.

New-wave research is trying to involve respondents as partners rather than objects of observation. Recruit a diverse group of creative minds and have a conversation with them – this is the way to go, as opposed to old-fashioned 'clocking-in' research.

Types of research

In simple terms, there's **'quantitative research,'** which involves recruiting large panels of customers that can comprise:

- Ad hoc work to investigate a market.
- Tracking studies (such as Target Group Index or Taylor Nelson's shopper studies).
- Online research, such as that popularised by YouGov.co.uk.
- Brand purchase and stocking trends (Nielsen).
- Brand-switching studies that show how many people change brands, how often and precisely when – a way of measuring the power of marketing activity (Nielsen or GKK).
- Advertising research – day-after recall work and effectiveness studies on a broader front done by people such as Millward Brown.
- Major government-funded social and economic studies.
- Market studies such as those produced by Mintel.

And there's **'qualitative research'**, which commonly comprises:

- Focus groups (or group discussions) usually lasting two hours and comprising a moderator with seven or so specially recruited respondents.

● Depth interviews – one-to-one research work, typically an intensive hour's interview.

'Respected' research is expensive. By this I mean the sort of research private equity and investment banks like. But limit this if you can and spend your own money on understanding, provoking and advancing consumer ideas.

Good researchers are often the brightest and most exciting intellects you'll encounter in marketing and tend to be adept at benchmarking things such as advertising and new products. When a professional researcher says, 'In my experience ...' it usually pays to listen, especially if they're relaxed and 'off duty', because they have listened to an awful lot of people in their time.

Useful web sites are the Market Research Society, the market research national and international body which has two useful sites: www.mrs.org.uk and www.theresearchbuyersguide.com (I refer to this latter one later on). More is more when it comes to learning.

Good, investigative research leads to discoveries like the one Prius made about their solar panels and air-cooled snoozing drivers. Good research tells you a deodorant called 'No-Sweat' might work in Australia, but probably not so well elsewhere.

Trusting your own eyes and ears

But our mission is brilliance, not mediocrity, which is why I want to focus on some easy-to-set-up research techniques that can lead you personally to eureka moments. As Warren Buffett said:

'In the end I always believe my own eyes rather than something else.'

1 **Online questionnaires.** They are cheap to administer and once you have a reasonable sample of respondents you can get very fast responses to questions you have.

2   **Consumer-complaint chat rooms**. Robert Heller, the
    management guru, said his dilemma was that only one
    person in ten who had a complaint actually bothered to
    complain. He advocated soliciting complaints and dealing
    with them.

3   **Brand surgeries**. Brand surgeries come from the world
    of politics and are the way you, the brand steward, gets
    to meet your customers (your voters) and test out the
    temperature every now and again.

4   **Super-groups**. Consumer councils of reasonably expert
    people.

5   **What's new, pussycat?** This is about having a bunch of
    bright 'vigilantes' (vigilant people) who, just in the course
    of their normal lives, keep their eyes open for exciting
    innovations. The Dutch innovation watchers called
    Trendwatching (the B2C division) and their B2B division,
    Springwise, have 8,000 trend spotters.

> But if you want to know
> what's going on in a
> market go out and talk
> to people.

But if you want to know what's going
on in a market go out and talk to
people. What could be simpler? It
may not be objective but it'll get you
thinking.

How to choose brilliant research companies

● You want the best brains. So the first question is how smart
  are they? Only the best will help you to be brilliant and they
  MUST be great at speaking in simple, easy-to-understand
  language.

● They must bring insights to what you are doing that provide
  exceptional value.

● They must have track records in your area so they can
  benchmark their observations against competition.

- Ask to see them at work before you hire them. Everyone has a right to test-drive an expensive sports car, which is what they are like.
- Avoid big and boring. Contact www. theresearchbuyersguide.com to find out who's doing good stuff right now.
- And better still choose a brilliant person, not a company ... someone who will tell you the truth. There are lots of good people around. Ask other marketers.

▶ brilliant examples

Lampposts and babies. Butch Rice (a South African marketing consultant) played a game whereby he produced a graph showing the relationship between the number of babies born and the number of lampposts in the world. He sought to show (quite bogusly, of course) that birth rate was lamppost-dependent. Whereas the number of lampposts actually indicates density of population. One of the best examples of ludicrous correlations you could find, this is an excellent example of lies, damned lies and statistics.

In getting people to support a charity there are three rules. One, you must ask and ask and ask. Two, you must be pleasant and clear. Three, you must make it easy to respond. In the recently published book *Yes!* by Goldstein, Martin and Cialdini, they described how they'd researched the difference between asking for a donation for the American Cancer Society with and without this line: 'even a penny would help'. Donations with that line were 50 per cent, without it 29 per cent. QED: the case for using research well.

The pros and cons of research

Research is a vital tool in brilliant marketing, but it is a chisel and sometimes your brilliance has been to create a beautiful marketing mahogany table. Be careful how you use one on the other.

Real brilliance comes from a passionate interest in people and a desire to know how they tick. It also comes from the realisation that many people change their minds, their habits and nearly 40 per cent of them their partners.

1 **Research has drawbacks.** It works on what has happened in the past – it is poor at trying to see the future and the really big things like life, death, fire and wheels.

2 **Think hard before you do paid-for research** – DIY research is a great place to learn.

3 **But if you do, only use the best, brightest researchers.** Too much work is done by low-grade moderators working with respondents who are groupies, spending most of their lives in sitting rooms in group discussions. Ask yourself if you'd trust these people to tell you how to run your life.

> Good research can provide you with great insights.

4 **Research is a radar system.** Good research can provide you with great insights – look out for the insights, not the whole truth.

5 **Use your own ears and eyes too.** Make sure you have your own conduits to consumers. You cannot be a brilliant marketer unless you have a direct line to enough people who use and understand your brand.

6 **Are your key customers committed to your brand?** The key in building a brilliant brand is to find as many people as you can who are really committed to it, not just loyal but who actually adore it.

PART 5

Marketing in small businesses or doing it for yourself

'm not against big businesses. I'm a fan of Google and Apple (who couldn't be?). I'm in love with the spirit Nike had in the period of their pre-21st-century glory. I love the confidence with which companies such as Diageo, Heinz and Ford go about what they do. I was in awe of the creativity and focus of Mazda and Panasonic. But there's something about big companies that's beginning to worry me quite a lot.

It's that being big makes you a bully and makes you go prematurely deaf. Being big makes you think 'There's my way and then there's my way.' Most of all, being big makes you an enemy of marketing. The big decisions you make will be about downsizing, consolidating and acquisitions. They should be about marketing decisions but they won't be.

brilliant tip

If you get too big to focus on marketing, give up.

Small businesses are about the future. They are about innovation. They are about learning. They are about being busy doing important things – sometimes too busy. And if they have a problem it's that sometimes they're so busy they don't spend enough time focusing on their most important assets: their customers and their marketing.

CHAPTER 23

Watching
people is
what great
marketing
needs

S mall businesses need walking Geiger counters as bosses, people who are their own market researchers, smelling, sensing and hearing the sound of the market. Simon Marks of M&S used to tour the stores on a Saturday listening to the sound of the tills. Steve Jobs used to go on his hands and knees in car parks examining Mercedes and BMW fenders.

Shops, high streets and trade shows

Walk high streets and shopping centres – get a feel for what's going on. Go to trade shows and when you've researched where's best and worked out how to operate there, show at one. As an exhibitor said recently, 'Big distributors go to these events in a buying mood, or at least in a looking mood.' As a small business your most important assets are nimble-footedness, a curiosity of spirit and an irrepressible desire to learn. Feed that desire by keeping close to your market.

brilliant tip

In a small business a day spent shopping counts as working.

Drink inspiration

Stay inspired by reading, surfing the web, talking, thinking, trying new ideas. Clare Blampied, MD of Saclà (the top-of-the-range

Italian sauce maker that has just celebrated 20 years in the UK), finds her inspiration as a 24/7/365 ambassador for the brand. Someone as enthusiastic and responsive to new ideas is wasted in an office and needs to spend their life listening, laughing and spreading the good news about their brand. She's good at all three. And she isn't running a small business – it turns over about £30 million – but she behaves as though it is.

> All brilliant marketers need to stick to detail and never stop pitching their stories.

Which is what all good businesses do: think big and act small. Lesson: All brilliant marketers need to stick to detail and never stop pitching their stories about their business. It's inspiring to hear and creates an inspiration loop.

Do you really know your real customers?

I was quite polite about research earlier. But, like MBAs and HR, old-fashioned research has become too much about process and that ghastly expression 'checking for negatives'. Some leaders of companies avoid research because they think they know better, some because it's so expensive, but there's a better reason. Research is a lens through which we see the past, what people think top-of-mind or what they think we want to hear. Here's what business start-up and head of HotSquash (www.hotsquash. com) Darren Sydnick said: 'It's crucial to plan but I planned far too much. Get out there with your product, get feedback and test your segmentation. F*** the research companies who offer focus groups!! Just speak to people.' (Darren is not given to bad language. So he must have really meant it.)

brilliant tip

Eschew research. Just speak to people. (I promise 'eschew' isn't rude.)

Look for the problems – the niggle points

Things that slightly irritate you are corrosive in the end. As Richard Brown, managing partner of Cognosis, the management consultancy, put it, 'It's the gap in a market where creativity is', and that gap is often the irritation gap. Examples: unusually nice beer glasses like Peroni's do 'brand wonders' and make up for those ordinary glasses that make going out feel like going down. Example: not knowing when the next bus is coming now solved by 'arrival-time due boards' – puts buses back on the map. Example: *The Times* discount scheme whereby grumpy 'as an "austerity measure" I'll stop taking *The Times* at £400 or so a year' is transformed into my being a lifetime customer (for the time being) at £250 or so instead.

brilliant tip

You get to identify niggle points by watching people, and when they swear under their breath a lot you may have a winning strategy before you.

It's the little things

Ever since the Betty Crocker cake-mix brand was transformed by a bit of interactive advice – 'just add an egg' (previously, with the egg included, no one wanted to buy it) – it's been clear that the little things can swing the votes. Politics enlightens us. One headline can do it.

So what are your little things? This book is about the big thing of marketing. So I asked Simon Woodhead, the founder of one of Britain's newest vineyards, Stopham, 'How much of your time has been spent on marketing as opposed to production and other stuff?' His reply chilled me and thrilled me too:

'Not much ... we've focused on getting the best-quality grapes and

wine. The distribution and customers have resulted from this quality.
We've also been lucky with contacts. And there's a buzz around
English wine right now.'

Thrillingly self-confident in one of the most competitive markets
I know, and thrillingly right in asserting the key need to get the
product right, it's also chilling because he highlights the big issue
for new businesses – pressure of time and focus.

Lesson: No one can beat a pathway to your door if they don't
know you are there with a great product. (But Jane MacQuitty of
The Times calls the Pinot Gris 'a triumph', so well done.)

brilliant tip

Spend enough time to create a great product – and then market it
like mad … non-stop … with stories, creativity and fun.

Never-ending conversations

Get around you as many people as you can who make you laugh,
think and think again. You need a mentor if you're a new business. You need a bouncing board and someone you can moan to.
And it's easier in retail or the restaurant business because that's
what your customers do the whole time. Good local restaurants
build unspoken partnerships with loyal customers – very much
a zeitgeist relationship in marketing.

If you can balance
service and product
you'll win.

What I love is when you can go off-
menu and get what you want without
a word – 'Hi Paula, can Peter knock
me up a plain omelette that's nice
and runny?' There's a restaurant like
that round the corner in Brighton called Blenio's, with a Roux
Brothers-trained chef, that has the best front-of-house in Britain.
If you can balance service and product like this you'll win.

How tough can it get?

However tough it gets, the people best placed to deal with it are going to be small, nimble and flexible. They are going to be businesses that listen to their customers. Their resilience and good humour are vital. No one wants to buy from a miserable, surly malcontent. The next time a taxi driver says 'It's a recession, mate, it's over and I blame them Poles,' say 'I feel sick. Stop the cab at once and let me out.'

brilliant tip

Always try to be in a brilliantly upbeat mood. This is one of your most potent marketing tools.

One of the toughest sectors is the charity world, where you are dependent on altruism and social need to survive. Petit Miracle trains homeless and unemployed people (many of them women) to do interior design and learn the skills to enable them to give a flat the individuality and style of its occupant. Everyone deserves the chance to learn something aspirational, useful and life-enhancing. Tough as things will always be for the Petit Miracles of this world, having a vision and a reason for carrying on pitching your good idea is what makes charities specifically, and small businesses in general, so rewarding. Keep the faith and keep trying to show that your work can transform lives.

Marketing by showing what you can do

We keep on reading about the need for unexpected moments of generosity or sampling of products. If you are trying to sell musical instruments or high-ticket items such as electric organs, the smart people lend them to a prospective purchaser to try and see if they like them. (Hopefully they'll fall so hopelessly in love they won't want to be parted from them.) Sample your wares.

Do speculative work so potential customers see what you can do. A designer I know called Jess Wood, who set up and runs A Little Zest, did this. 'Have a look at these' she said and hopefully something good will happen as the person to whom they were presented for free was knocked out by the gesture.

First impressions are critical

We are in the perception business in marketing. We add value by making people perceive something that's ordinary as being extraordinary. In that respect we are economic magicians. Nowhere is that more important than in that first moment people come across you in an advertisement, or on the web, or in your shop. Nicole Urbanski opened a boutique in Brighton in October 2011. First impressions? Well, like Helena Rubinstein, I could smell success. It was minimalist and confident. My wife loves it. What was interesting is Nicole has managed to make a clothes shop feel like a very upmarket delicatessen.

> Give people a taste that makes them want more.

The lesson is to take advantage of that first moment and give people a canapé of your offering – a taste that makes them want more. At that first-impression moment all businesses are in the same place, regardless of their size.

Love your customers

Margaret Heffernan, in her book *Women on Top*, explains one of the reasons why in the USA female entrepreneurs are twice as likely as their male counterparts to succeed. They have an unquestioning, almost unreasonable love of their customers. And customers need it. They need to be listened to, stroked and, yes, challenged. A PR company in Reading with a long list of clients, called C8, does that but their acid test is keeping in constant touch with them. Their MD is a never-still client-stroker, 24/7 asking: Are you OK, is there anything you need?

Successful marketing on a small scale

Being small means you can focus. It means you can become a real expert. Stories such as those listed below are not so uncommon. What these young entrepreneurs are discovering is if you have a good idea don't just try it; go for it. But also market it well to your target audience. Name and presentation count:

1 **Trevillion Images** is in the business of finding great and original images for book covers. They are innovative, international and specialist.

2 **Jibbitz loved Crocs** (those brightly coloured casual shoes) so they focused on creating decorations for Crocs – charms and that sort of thing. So successful were they that Crocs bought them.

3 **'Debbie & Andrew's'** sausages from Harrogate are the best sausages I've tasted. Originally the brand was called 'Manor Born', but the redesign of the brand (giving eponymous craft credentials) won them a Design Council award and hugely increased sales before being acquired.

4 **Linda Owen-Lloyd runs 'Children's Book Illustrations'** because, she says, 'that's what we know best'. (Isn't that great?)

5 **The world of youthful developers of apps for**

smartphones, doing it for fun and earning perhaps 75p an app sold, are finding to their surprise that their pocket money has in consequence leapt to £50,000.

CHAPTER 24

Small-business marketing checklist

1 What are the three things you could improve?
The quest to improve must be endless. Constantly ask what needs fixing, what needs improving, what you can afford and what you can't afford not to change.

> The quest to improve must be endless.

2 How do you measure up?
Put yourself in a 'critical' customer's place and compare yourself with your competitors – the people most likely to take business from you. Are you making the most of your strengths?

3 What's your current business like?
How are sales, repeat sales and conquest sales? What's the mood amongst your customers? How can you work with this and make your offering more relevant for now?

4 What do your stakeholders think?
Your suppliers, investors, distributors, staff and friends ... what do they think? Listen to their observations.

5 Who are your customers, current and potential?
Are you looking after them brilliantly, do they feel valued? Where are the next customers? How are you going to reach them?

6 What are your current marketing initiatives?
I'm presuming there's only going be a good, short, focused
list. Are you happy they are as impactful as they should be?
What haven't you tried that you should have?

**7 What are you planning to do next to make a
difference?**
Sneaky question, but if it forces you to think ahead about
what will make the real difference, that's good. In small
businesses it's hard to stand back. Try it. What would it
take to be twice the size or twice as profitable?

**8 What are the people who talk about you and your
market saying?**
Talk to a journalist who knows about your sector and get
their perspective. What could change your market? What
factors exist that could transform or destroy it?

**9 What's new that you've seen recently and want to
emulate?**
This may not necessarily be in your own market. Some of
the best ideas come from people taking a good idea from
one place and putting it in another.

10 If you could start again what would you do differently?
This is the test of whether you are learning enough. You
need to be creative, self-confident, proud of what you do
and energetic. You also have to be
smart enough to learn from failure
and the things that aren't working
out quite right.

> Learn from failure and
> the things that aren't
> working out quite right.

Running your own business, making
a product you are proud of and turning this into a brand that
you love are a great way to spend your life. Learning how to be a
non-stop marketer of it is what will make the biggest difference
of all. And be the most fun.

PART 6

A summary of the marketing rules

The trouble with rules is the rebel in me wants to break them. And the trouble with summaries is they can make you wonder why you bothered to read the whole book. Go to the summary and all is revealed. Go to the end of the book and find the butler did it. Job done. But it's not that simple. Marketing in this book is a thriller. The book is not simply a textbook. There are twists and turns. The story of modern marketing is the story of changing humanity. Underpinning it are some basic axioms and these are contained here. Useful to know but, rather like the rules of golf, on their own they won't help you be a better player. Most important is to focus on four things: the customer, the product, the marketing plan and the brand. And, as I say, if you are a small business then keep the good news coming, because with luck you'll break a few rules and the future will be yours.

CHAPTER 25

The Marketing Commandments

This is not so much an executive summary as a statement of those things marketers have to ensure happens in their heads and in their actions when they embark on a marketing campaign. I rather suppose Moses, had he lived today, would have brought down laminates rather than tablets of stone from Mount Sinai, or even a PowerPoint presentation. We're going to settle for paper.

The five things that matter most are:

1 The customer or consumer.

2 The product or service.

3 The weapons available with which to go and market.

4 The issue of branding.

5 What you the smaller marketer do, as you are the future.

The Ten Customer Commandments

1 Remember, they are right (even when you think they are wrong).

2 Spend as much time as you can listening to them and to as many different types of them as possible.

3 Give them unexpected treats to say 'thank you' for being loyal – never take them for granted.

4 Never stop wooing them and romancing your brand.

5 Try and find out those little things in life that irritate them.

6 Understand how people are different and why and how to work with this so you can fix them.

> When you make a mistake say 'sorry' and put it right.

7 When you make a mistake say 'sorry' and put it right.

8 Ask them to introduce you to their friends.

9 Always be faithful to them and their changing needs.

10 Love your consumer as though you were married to them.

The customers who buy your product or service come first. Without them and their support nothing will happen. Your love affair with them and the way in which you woo and look after them will determine your success. And remember your customer is always right. Even when they are wrong.

> Remember your customer is always right. Even when they are wrong.

The Ten Product or Service Commandments

1 Be better value than your competitor ... make it easy to buy you.

2 Be simpler. Cut out the unnecessary knobs and switches.

3 Solve points of irritation, those things in a process or product sector that really rile people.

4 Constantly change and improve ... never stop trying to get better.

5 Spread your appeal to your consumers. Can you extend your portfolio by price or function and reach more people?

6 Be easy – use simple language and don't package your product so people can't get at it or understand it.

7 Be fast. Speed is an advantage. Next-day delivery. Call back/email back in hours, not days.

8 Merchandise your successes. Tell people how well it's going. Make them feel part of a 'success club'.

9 Be irrational about quality. If you spot a problem, stop it. Never ship sub-standard products.

10 Love your own product. Are you really proud of it?

If you don't have a fetish about your product or service, if you aren't constantly trying to see how to make it better or easier to use, then you aren't serving the interests of the consumer or your business. Too little is written about product. If your product isn't good enough there's only so much your marketing can do to help you.

The Ten Marketing-Weapon Commandments

1 You need to find an advertising idea that you love and that cuts through, even if you can't afford to spend money on advertising (yet). It'll be the soul of your sales pitch.

2 You need to create fact-based interesting stories the whole time to maintain PR momentum.

3 If your web site isn't wonderful that's a problem. They are relatively low cost to create now. It mostly needs your time and creativity. This is your first priority.

4 Social and word of mouth are the low-cost ways of spreading your good word. But if you find it hard to focus on Twitter, build a conversational base to start with. Do not try selling.

5 Sponsorship is expensive to do well but can sometimes be a magic solution.

6 Do you really love the design of your product and its packaging? If not fix it.

7 Direct marketing in the form of e-letters, fliers and one-to-one presentations can work brilliantly if you do them brilliantly. Otherwise don't.

8 Customer-relationship marketing and selling are at the centre of any marketing plan. Your customers make your business. Are you spending enough time listening to them?

9 Buzz and experiential: the way to put sex appeal at low cost into your marketing. But don't do it unless you believe it really makes £1 look like £10.

10 Pulling it all together is the trick. Balance budget against the key deliverables. Don't try and do too much. Focus the bulk of your spend on what is most important to your plan.

These weapons, powerful as they are, won't work unless there's a strong central idea holding them together: something that is distinctive, memorable and that makes a competitive claim. Your problem is breadth of choice – what you can afford in relation to what will do the job. It's your decision. The trick is to keep it very simple. Be bold but not too tricky.

> The trick is to keep it very simple.

The Ten Branding Commandments

1 What do you want people to think, feel and like about your brand?

2 Give your brand a personality ... think of it as a real thing itself, not just a product. Imagine your whole reputation was sunk into it. It's that important.

3 And a two- or three-word equity. For example: authentic, Venezuelan chocolate. For example: real bikers' oil. A summary claim of your specialness.

4 Give it a great name or your name. Don't end up with a willowy, forgettable nothing.

5 Money spent on design won't be wasted. Ever. If your designer understands what you are looking for your brand to be like he may astound you.

6 Use your instincts. This is gut time, not brain time.

7 Look at what other great brands do ... borrow, steal, imitate and be inspired by them.

8 Be ambitious. Why not? Dream a little. Imagine what success might be like and how you might get there.

9 Attitude wins. Attitude is your red thread...what you really believe in ... what you'd die for.

10 Brands are worth money. Much more money than products. That alone makes this value-adding process fun. It also makes it expensive for lesser beings to compete with you.

The Holy Grail of marketing lies in branding. Create a brand, develop a brand and discover the amazing added value in intangibles you've been responsible for. Brands are sexy. Brands have a desirability that's far greater than a simple product. But when you have a brand, rather like a splendid plant, you have to water and nourish it. Brands are the virtual pets of marketing.

> The Holy Grail of marketing lies in branding.

The Ten Small Commandments (for small businesses)

1 You've got to have a great product of which you're really proud. Just 'OK' is no good.

2 Be obsessed with detail. Little things make a huge difference and small businesses can get this right.

3 Do everything you do as though it was a 'big show' – be theatrical, not meek.

4 Love your brand obsessively. This is your life.

5 You are a nimble lightweight; pity the slow-moving overweights. Never underestimate the benefits of the speed and flexibility you can offer.

6 Think big; act small. No one need know how small you really are. That's where web sites offer a vast plus to small businesses.

7 Spend half your time on your product; half your time on your marketing of it.

8 Spend lots of time talking to your customers. Always have something interesting and new to say.

9 Run a transparent business – avoid springing nasty surprises (especially on investors or banks).

10 Keep the good news coming – we all want you to win and read about you winning.

Being small is where Apple and Microsoft started. Heinz and Ford both went bust a few times before they got it right. Being small is being in control of your own destiny. Be mean and keen. You won't get rich fast but if it goes well, who knows? In the meantime, market that great little brand of yours with all the energy you have, making every single penny really count.

The final say

1 **Watch the money**. Having little money often means having to be very resourceful. Be very careful with money. Pay your bills. Don't be unkind to suppliers but look at every £ on the basis of its being your duty as a marketer to multiply its impact and get a great return on investment.

2 **Inspire the creativity**. This is the 'magic marketing juice': the nutrient that turns a good idea into a brilliant idea. This is where you must be utterly unreasonable. If what you have got or are given isn't brilliant, try again and again and again and again until something special happens.

Unless you can achieve brilliance in marketing you'll fail. There's too much noise in our lives. And there are too many products and too many companies to choose from. As with our schools, anything rated less than 'outstanding' stands for nothing at all.

What did you think of this book?

We're really keen to hear from you about this book, so that we can make our publishing even better.

Please log on to the following website and leave us your feedback.

It will only take a few minutes and your thoughts are invaluable to us.

www.pearsoned.co.uk/bookfeedback

Index